# GROWTH
## A NEW VISION FOR THE
# SUNDAY SCHOOL

CHARLES ARN
DONALD McGAVRAN
WIN ARN

PUBLISHED BY
Church Growth Press
150 S. LOS ROBLES, #600
PASADENA, CA. 91101

# DEDICATION

These pages are dedicated to church school teachers, that great army of Christians who week by week pray, plan, and teach . . . giving unselfishly of themselves for the advancement of Christ's Kingdom.

It is our sincere hope and prayer that this book will be an important key for these teachers in unlocking new horizons of possibility, effectiveness, and growth.

2nd Printing 1981

Published by Christian Communication
150 South Los Robles, #600, Pasadena, CA 91101

Printed in U.S.A.

Library of Congress Catalog Card No. 79-66211
ISBN 0-93440-8-03-3

# CONTENTS

# FOREWORD

It would be hard to be more excited about a book for the church than I am about this one. I'm a Christian today because of a Sunday School that had as its goal, reaching and winning every unchurched person in the community. I know, because I was one of those people who were reached. My commitment to Christ and the church is a direct result of Sunday School teachers who loved me, cared for me and for my family, introduced me to Jesus Christ, and began a program of discipling me in the faith.

Because of the vision of this church scores of people in my neighborhood became Christians. We grew together, with the church as the center of our lives. Many of us are still close friends thirty years later.

In this book, Charles Arn, Donald McGavran, and Win Arn state an objective and vision for the Sunday School that I hope every pastor, Christian Education director, Sunday School teacher and class member in America catches. It is a vision of the Sunday School growing as a total, integrated program of evangelism, discipleship, fellowship, and training laity of all ages in the local church. And so it must be. The growing Sunday School is alive and reaching out and meeting needs in every age group, for every kind of person the local church ministers to.

This vision of growth rings true to my own Christian heritage and spiritual development.

The goal of growth rings true to the Word of God and Christ's call to the church to go . . . and make disciples.

And the strategies of growth outlined in this book ring true in the vast experience of these authors and church growth professionals about how Sunday Schools grow.

I sincerely hope and pray that more people in local churches will have the opportunity to attend a Sunday School characterized by attributes described in the chapters that follow.

*Robert C. Screen, layperson*

CHAPTER ONE

# GROWTH: THE BEGINNINGS

What are your early memories of Sunday School?

I remember being in a classroom with eight other junior high boys, sitting around a small circle in a cramped, antiquated room. As boys of that age do, we pushed, shoved, punched, whispered, and talked . . . until the class was in constant bedlam. Our teacher, a middle-aged woman weighing over 200 pounds, with a warm expression and friendly eyes, always taught with a large, well-worn Bible open across her knees. We knew very little about her as a person except that her husband had died some years before and her only son had been injured in a high school football accident which left him a lifetime cripple.

Though I can't recall a single lesson or illustration from the class, I do remember Sunday after Sunday being asked to sit beside my teacher, where I was assigned the task of holding her ruler, pencil, lesson sheets, Bible . . . anything to keep me occupied. Looking back, the special attention must have been founded on her conclusion that I was the chief troublemaker. Eventually, promotion time came and the class moved to another room and another teacher.

The next meeting with my junior high teacher came some years later and quite by chance.

In the intervening years, I had completed high school, served as an officer in the military, returned to finish college, and at the time was in seminary preparing for the ministry. During my first summer as a seminarian, I was working at a Bible conference center where one of my responsibilities was to meet incoming buses, welcome arriving passengers and direct them to their rooms.

The incident is still vivid in my mind!

A large yellow bus arrived. The double doors opened and slowly down the steps came my junior high Sunday School teacher. She had aged, but her wrinkled face was still warm and friendly. Reaching the last step, she looked up and saw me. She remembered! With tears flowing down her cheeks, she hugged me with a 200-pound hug and between sobs kept repeating, "It was worth it all . . . It was worth it all."

The Sunday School played an important part in bringing me to faith and discipleship, as it has played an important part in the lives of countless others. Who can deny that since its inception, some 200 years ago, the Sunday School movement has been greatly blessed by God for winning and nuturing people in the faith?

## RELIGIOUS INSTRUCTION— OUR STRONG ROOTS IN YESTERDAY

### . . . Early Foundations

When you next meet in your Sunday School class, pause to reflect on your rich heritage. As a teacher or participant in your church's adult or children's classes, you are a part of a tradition dating back thousands of years.

The Old Testament and early Jewish records reflect the great emphasis the Hebrews put on teaching. The Shema, as the Hebrews referred to Deuteronomy 6:4-9, was God's command to "teach diligently unto thy children" the words of Moses: "And thou shalt love the Lord thy God with all thy soul and with all thy might."

The spirit of the modern teacher stood with these early Hebrews, as they sought to make the teachings of the law their guiding force in everyday life. The Jewish teacher, called Rabbi, was accorded great honor in every Jewish community. The rabbi and the synagogue are recognized today as having an important influence on the educational process of modern Christianity,[1] and many scholars believe the synagogue services distinctly foreshadowed the early Sunday School.[2]

Jesus of Nazareth also participated in the religious instruction of His day as He learned, and later taught, in the synagogue schools. The Jewish educational system, of which Jesus was a part, decreed that children ages 5 through 10 learn the law, beginning with Leviticus, and then the history of the Jewish people. From age 10 to 15, pupils were taught the unwritten Jewish traditions. At age 15, students were considered old enough to ask questions, to dispute with the doctors, and to attend the higher schools.[3] As with other Jewish boys, Jesus' early habits included attending the synagogue on the Sabbath (Luke 4:16), and learning of His religious heritage through such instruction.

In His earthly ministry Jesus used teaching to communicate the truth. While John the Baptist is spoken of as a preacher, Jesus is most often recalled as a teacher.[4] In fact, "teacher" is used 42 times in the Gospels with reference to Jesus, and another 47 times He is spoken of as "teaching." The Sermon on the Mount is introduced by Matthew (5:2) with the words: "He opened his mouth and *taught* them . . ."

Jesus always followed His exhorting and evangelizing with teaching.[5] The very nature of His mission as the Messiah required that He teach concerning the Kingdom of God. Without such teaching, His Gospel would probably have been grossly misunderstood and His mission defeated altogether.[6] Jesus' command to his followers—to make disciples—was to be implemented, in part, by teaching: "Go, therefore, and make disciples of all nations . . . *teaching* them to observe whatsoever I have commanded you . . ." (Matt. 28:19, 20). We often call Jesus the greatest teacher who ever lived—a teacher whose influence has exceeded that of all others.

The apostles were obedient to the command to carry on Christ's teaching. They taught everywhere, using every possible occasion to make known the truth they had received. The rapid spread of Christianity was a direct result of both *evangelizing* and *teaching*. In spirit, the modern teacher stood with the great Apostle Paul as he taught believers and non-believers about the way of salvation. He and Barnabas spent much time in Antioch teaching (Acts 11:26; 15:35). Paul taught in Corinth a year and a half (Acts 18:11), and spent his last years in Rome devoting himself to "teaching those things which concern the Lord Jesus Christ . . ." (Acts 28:31).

## . . . Into Later Generations

The roots of Christian education extend from the Old and New Testament periods, and continue on through the growth of the early church.

By the end of the first century, Christianity had grown so rapidly that new converts and children of the believers needed more systematic instruction in their faith. Perhaps the earliest formal school for Christian teaching was in Alexandria—a theological seminary for adults to learn more about the faith. One of the graduates of this seminary was a young man named Origen.

In spirit, the modern teacher was with Origen in 203 A.D. as he went into the city of Alexandria to gather children from the many churches and organize them into groups of instruction, called catechetical schools (schools teaching the principles of Christianity).[7] The purpose was preparation for church membership, and the curriculum was the doctrines of the church and history of their faith. Some historians suggest that I Corinthians 15:3-5, and other similar passages, may have been the primitive creed used to instruct these young candidates for baptism, and then recited by new church members as their confession of faith.[8]

These catechetical schools soon spread throughout Christendom. The excavation of many early churches indicates that provisions were often made for such classrooms. Records indicate that in the first centuries, during the rapid spread of the church, the teaching was often done by laity—both men and women.[9] With this active involvement of the Christian laity, the faith continued to spread rapidly. Christian education of adults and children was a significant means of spreading the faith, both for instructing and for incorporating people into the church.

But as the Dark Ages rolled across Europe, the schools for religious instruction, found during the first centuries in nearly every church, began to disappear. Religious teaching gravitated to the cities, the great cathedrals, and to the monasteries. Education was limited to the monks and the clergy, and any religious learning by laity was looked upon with suspicion. In the eighth century, Charlemagne attempted to establish village schools taught by clergy, but many of the clergy, themselves, were sadly deficient in Christian knowledge. Only in the monasteries was religious instruction preserved and passed on. Christian education for the common man had become almost non-existent.

### . . . A Fresh Breeze

The Protestant Reformation brought a breath of fresh air to religious instruction, and ushered in the concept of "the priesthood of all believers" and the role of laity. In 1524, Martin Luther, the great German reformer, prepared his first catechism for children and called attention to the need for religious instruction for all. He saw that the young and old alike must learn the Scriptures if religious truth was to belong to the common man. Luther's catechisms proved to be an effective way to communicate biblical truth to the people. Translations of the Bible into the language of the people, and the invention of the printing press were also major steps forward for Christian education and the growth of the church.

Across the Atlantic, in the American colonies, an increasing interest in religious instruction was growing as the catechetical method of teaching helped spread these new ideas of the Reformation to the laity.[10] Textbooks in American schools abounded with religious teaching. The recollection of a student who attended an early American school was recorded in 1642: "The teacher continually prayed with us and catechized us every week."[11] The Rev. C. Howie, minister at Oxford, Pennsylvania, reported in May, 1738, that he "examined the children every Lord's day in the church catechism."[12]

Such famous catechisms as the Heidelberg, the Westminster, and the Anglican Catechism represented the renewed importance church leaders were giving to religious instruction. Yet, even through the enlightened days of the Reformation, it was still the clergy who were the instructors. Religious education was limited to the catechetical method, and instruction was restricted to the bounds of the parish and the availability of a local clergyman.[13]

## A NEW EXPERIMENT—THE SUNDAY SCHOOL

Perhaps readers of this book would never be in a Bible study class taught by a lay person if a providential event had not taken place 200 years ago.

In a back alley of Gloucester, England, in 1780, Robert

Raikes gathered a group of poor, uneducated children to hold the first session of a Sunday School class.

Considered the father of the modern Sunday School, Raikes was a man to whom the sight of pain, poverty, misery, and hunger was a constant burden. The physical, intellectual, and moral conditions of the people in Raikes' day were deplorable. In the industrial cities, such as Gloucester, conditions were especially bad. The poor tried to survive on inadequate diets, they lived in inadequate houses, they wore inadequate clothing. Few common people had the privilege of any formal education. No public schools existed, and most of the poor people were totally illiterate.

For years, Raikes championed the needs of these people, but saw few results. After nearly 25 years of failure to eliminate the problems, he decided to try what he called "a new experiment." In Gloucester, the neglected, ragged children worked in the factories during the week. On Sunday they played, quarreled, cursed, and fought in the streets. Realizing the uselessness of appealing to the parents, Raikes decided the vice, filth, corruption, and poverty could and must be combated through teaching children.

In 1780, he opened his first Sunday School in "Sooty Alley," named because of the chimney sweeps who lived there. His pupils were from the lowest levels of society and from places of the worst reputation. Some were so unwilling to go to Sunday School that he marched them there with logs tied to their feet so they could not escape.

The first Sunday Schools in England were established and conducted by people outside the church, and were designed to teach basic reading and writing skills. Any religious value of the Sunday Schools was incidental; their purpose was moral and educational. As the movement spread and some of the schools sought to meet in chapels and church rooms, they began to attract the attention of the clergy. Many clergy regarded such use of their buildings to be an "act of abomination." The Sunday School, in particular, was considered a dangerous and demoralizing agent of the devil. *The Gentlemen's Magazine* called the Sunday School "subversive of . . . that peace and tranquility which constitute the happiness of society; and that far from deserving encouragement and applause, it merits our contempt."[14]

The Archbishop of Canterbury called his bishops together to consider what should be done to stop the movement. William Pitt thought seriously of introducing a bill in Parliament to suppress the Sunday School. In Scotland, teaching on the Sabbath by laymen was pronounced a violation of the Fourth Commandment. Those who fostered schools among the poor were condemned and their teachers persecuted by the church.

But the opposition only served to attract attention to the Sunday School movement and the great need which existed for the work it was doing. John Wesley, one of the few churchmen who openly supported Raikes and his new Sunday School, recognized this new institution as "one of the noblest instruments which has been seen in Europe for some centuries, and will increase more and more."[15] In this confidence, Wesley, the founder of Methodism, adopted the Sunday School as an integral part of his own great undertaking and thus assured the growth of this new institution.

A few years after Raikes' "new experiment" had gained the attention of Europe, and a slow-growing degree of support from the church, the concept of the Sunday School was brought to America. Conditions were so different across the Atlantic, however, that the schools were much different from those in the English cities. For one, the appalling conditions of destitution and neglect were not found in American villages. For another, the Sunday School concept was introduced in America under the auspices and support of the church.

Wesley continued to espouse the Sunday School in America and was a major force in successfully transplanting it to the New World. In *The American Magazine,* he wrote, "Perhaps God may have a deeper end thereto than men are aware of. Who knows but what some of these schools may become nurseries for Christians?"[16] Wesley's foresight doubtless had much to do with the fact that Methodist churches in the United States were among the first to formally adopt the Sunday School as a regular part of their church work. This emphasis on the Sunday School undoubtedly contributed to the rapid growth of the Methodist Church, and resulted in the denomination becoming, at one time, the largest Protestant body in America.

One of the first official unions between the Sunday School and the organized church was in 1790 when the Methodist

Conference in Charleston, South Carolina, formally placed the Sunday School in the care of the church. It was ordered that there should be established

> . . . Sunday Schools in or near the place of worship. Let persons be appointed by the Bishops, Deacons, or Preachers to teach gratis all who will attend and have capacity to learn, from six o'clock in the morning till ten, and from two o'clock in the afternoon till six, when it does not interfere with public worship.[17]

The last ten years of the 18th century witnessed the formation of many Sunday Schools in cities of the United States, nearly all connected with churches. It was during this brief period that the concept of a teaching and writing school on Sunday according to the vision of Raikes, became distinct from the "Sunday School," recognized and adopted by the Church for the purpose of Christian instruction. This new approach to religious instruction meant that the Sunday School became, not a temporary expedient to rescue poor and ignorant children, but a permanent institution, discharging a specific and important new function in the life of the church.

Between 1827, when the Methodist Episcopal Church created an official Sunday School organization, and 1857, when the Southern Baptists incorporated the Sunday School into their denomination, most major Protestant groups endorsed the Sunday School and formally established organizational structures for its encouragement.

In modern times the Sunday School has become an important part of the transfer of the faith from generation to generation, providing personal growth, strength, and maturity to children, youth and adults.

The Sunday School movement was the opening of a new chapter in church history and a great new force for Christian education. Prior to the Sunday School, most clergy regarded themselves as the only qualified leaders for spiritual instruction, and were loathe to have "ignorant" laymen do any teaching at all. But modern concepts of the laity and their important role in Christian education have been immeasurably enlarged because of the "new experiment" called the Sunday School.

This view of active lay involvement in the Body is much more in accord with the vision of Christ and the practice of the early church than the clergy-dominated environment between A.D. 300 and A.D. 1800, prior to the rise of the Sunday School:

> In the New Testament church, the church was never understood as being led by the clergy, with the laity as second class members . . . .There are some who, of necessity, must give fulltime service in the church. But this makes them no more ministers in terms of quality or kind, than the so-called "Layman."[18]

The Sunday School brings unique advantages to the health and vitality of the local church. In American Protestant denominations today, 96% of all local churches have Sunday Schools, Sabbath Schools, or Church Schools.[19]

Christian education in your church is built on a rich heritage. If you are a teacher, you carry the torch held by tens of thousands of teachers before you, who have joyfully taught the faith to young and old. If you are a participant, you are one of millions who have been nourished and have grown through the inspired (and at times perhaps not-so-inspired!) teaching.

This book is especially for the teachers and Sunday School leaders who carry these great traditions into a challenging new age. It is a book dealing with tomorrow's Sunday School, Christian education, and church growth. It will help you look creatively and insightfully at how the ministry of teaching in your church can be effectively and significantly used by God for new growth and outreach in obedience to His command to "Go . . . teach . . . and make disciples!"

## FOOTNOTES

### CHAPTER ONE

1. Lewis J. Sherrill, *The Rise of Christian Education* (New York: MacMillan Co., 1950), p. 5.
2. Henry F. Cope, *The Evolution of the Sunday School* (Boston: Pilgrim Press, 1911), p. 8.
3. J. Edward Hakes, *An Introduction to Evangelical Christian Education* (Chicago: Moody, 1964), p. 26.
4. Sherrill, op. cit., p. 85.
5. Ibid., p. 87.
6. Ibid., p. 89.
7. Cope, op. cit., p. 23.
8. Sherrill, op. cit., p. 146.

9. Cope, op. cit., p. 25.
10. Clifton H. Brewer, *A History of Religious Education in the Episcopal Church to 1835* (New Haven: Yale University Press, 1904), p. 41.
11. Cope, op. cit., p. 61.
12. "Abstract of the Society for the Propagation of the Gospel" Proceedings 1733-34, p. 47.
13. Oscar S. Michael, *The Sunday School in the Development of the American Church,* 2nd edition (Milwaukee: The Young Churchman Company, 1918).
14. Cope, op. cit., p. 69
15. H.C. Trumbull, *Yale Lectures on the Sunday School* (Philadelphia: John D. Wattles, 1888), p. 118.
16. Cope, op. cit., pp. 71-72.
17. Ibid, p. 73.
18. Gene Getz, *Adult Education in the Church* (Chicago: Moody Press, 1970), p. 28.
19. Jacquet, Constant H. ed., *Yearbook of American and Canadian Churches 1979,* (Nashville: Abingdon, 1979), pp. 219-226.

# GROWTH: YESTERDAY, TODAY, AND TOMORROW ...MAYBE!

What about the Sunday School in the twentieth century? Sunday Schools and Christian education programs grew to become an accepted, even expected part of every local congregation. This century saw the Sunday School become the major teaching agency of the local church.

While every situation was different, we can watch the general trend by following one typical Sunday School from the turn of the twentieth century into the 1980s.

*Let's visit a Sunday School around the year 1914 . . .*

Sunday morning and you have just finished a delicious breakfast of eggs (68¢ a dozen), bacon (52¢ a pound), and milk (33¢ a half gallon), delivered by the milkman in his horse-drawn wagon at 5:00 a.m. this morning. The headlines of your morning paper read, "Tension in Europe Mounts."

Walking to church down a tree-lined street in your neighborhood, you are hurried along by the sound of the church bell. The church, architecturally, resembles a fortress with battlements around the tower. Parking space is no problem, for almost everyone walks to church. This is a neighborhood church in the true sense of the word, as neighbors see each other on Sunday and during the week.

Arriving at church, you climb the six entrance steps, walk through the large open doors, climb a second set of steps to enter the sanctuary. A Sunday School announcement board shows that the enrollment was 185 last week. Another sign points to stairs which lead to the basement where Sunday School classes will soon be assembling.

When you entered the church you were warmly welcomed and cordially invited to attend one of the Sunday School classes. The Sunday School, you learn, is centered around large classes for men and women . . . classes which do not intermix. There are six or seven classes from which you may choose, identified only by the name of the teacher. Age grading is not practiced. Fathers and sons, and mothers and daughters are usually in the same class. There are no classes exclusively for one particular group, such as young marrieds, singles, high school, or older adults.

Teachers are the focal point of the classes. These teachers are strong personalities, committed Christians, gifted men and women who teach the uniform lesson—a plan where everyone in the Sunday School studies the same scripture on the same Sunday. The class often takes the name of the teacher—the Frank Middleswart class or the Bertha Lawrence class. There is an intense loyalty to the teacher and to other members of the class. Many teachers serve in the same capacity for years and some make it "a lifetime calling."

You soon sense the evangelistic emphasis in the class. It is not unusual to ask for and expect decisions for Christ in the Sunday School classes. Lay teachers present the need for salvation . . . the way to be saved . . . and they lead class members into relationships with Jesus Christ. "Decision Sunday" is a regular part of the Sunday School when participants are given the opportunity to make a Christian commitment.

The music in the Sunday School is evangelistic and keeps the "flame burning brightly." Listen, they're singing now . . .

"You bring the one next to you;
and I'll bring the one next to me.
In no time at all
we'll have them all; so win them,
win them, one by one."

Members of the church usually come in through the Sunday School. It is in the Sunday School class that people are first welcomed, often converted, incorporated into a group, guided to a place of service, and received into church membership.

Enrollment in Sunday School is steadily growing, as the graph below indicates.

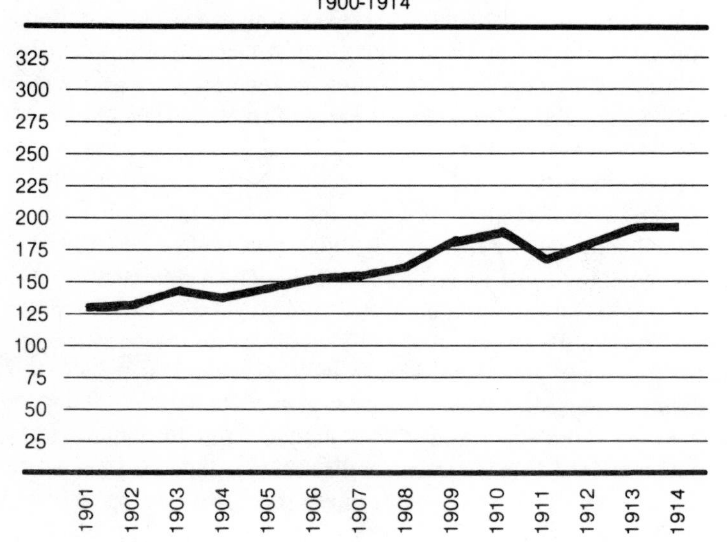


The opening exercises, led by the lay superintendent, are about to begin. He is going to recognize those who had birthdays last week and have them come forward to drop their birthday offering into the offering container. He will present a banner to the class with the best attendance . . .

*Now let's visit a Sunday School in the second third of the century, around, 1950 . . .*

Sunday morning, and you have just finished a delicious breakfast of eggs (60¢ a dozen), bacon (63¢ a pound), and milk (41¢ a half gallon), which were purchased at the neighborhood store the day before. The headlines of the morning paper read, "Truman orders MacArthur to Korea."

The music you hear as you drive to church comes from the newly-installed carillon in the bell tower. What changes are taking place! At the press of a button, recorded hymns emanate from the loudspeaker in the church tower. The old bell has been taken down and mounted as a memorial honoring one of the first families in the church. Members of this family still attend, but not as regularly as their parents did. About half of the church members still walk to church. Some have moved to the suburbs and now drive 10-20 minutes from their homes. Others have moved farther away and now attend different churches. Many of the members who attend on Sundays never see each other during the week, as the rise in personal mobility and the transportation boom has changed the meaning of the word "community."

Arriving at church, you are uncertain as to which class to attend, but you finally ask an older man whose coat displays pins for 25 years of perfect Sunday School attendance.

All the classes are now age-graded. The church recently employed a new director of religious education. As the number of marriages nationally has been increasing the church has formed married couples' classes such as "The Home Builders," "Happy Couples," and "The Wedded Band." There were objections to these classes by Frank Middleswart and other teachers, so they were allowed to keep their own classes; however, attendance has not been growing in their classes as much as in the others.

These new classes for couples are growing rapidly and are organized around a common area of interest—marriage. Class members share opinions on various topics and usually a coffee time follows. The teacher is much less the focal point, and close relationships develop among the couples in the class.

With the growing number of children, much emphasis is now directed on the youth department, and new children are being added to the enrollment. In fact, the term "Sunday School" is becoming more and more synonymous with religious education for children.

Because the Sunday School seems to be made up of similar kinds of people, classes are mostly oriented toward those people. Single people, since there are few in the Sunday School, are generally overlooked in curriculum planning, but can join one of the existing classes for couples if they wish.

There is a decrease in the evangelistic emphasis in the Sunday School. The focus is moving toward spiritual nurture of Christians.

Evangelism is seen as the work of the minister or specialists rather than of the lay teacher or class member. Periodically, a traveling evangelist holds meetings at the church, but evangelism is now thought of as an event, as the small sign in the front of the church indicates: "Special evangelistic service this Sunday evening 7:30 p.m."

The Sunday School is improving its methods. People now sit in a circle rather than in straight rows; filmstrips are occasionally used; periodically, a field trip is taken. Sunday School conventions are popular as a way of exchanging ideas on the latest teaching techniques and methods. The new religious education director is suggesting that the name "Sunday School" be changed to "Church School."

Growth in enrollment is taking place at an increasing rate, with little or no planning. The children of present church members regularly enroll, and Christian families moving into the area often join. Few notice, however, that the Sunday School is no longer attracting non-Christians in any significant number. But enrollment is now 273 and growing strong. Church membership has also been increasing.

**SUNDAY SCHOOL ATTENDANCE**
1915-1950

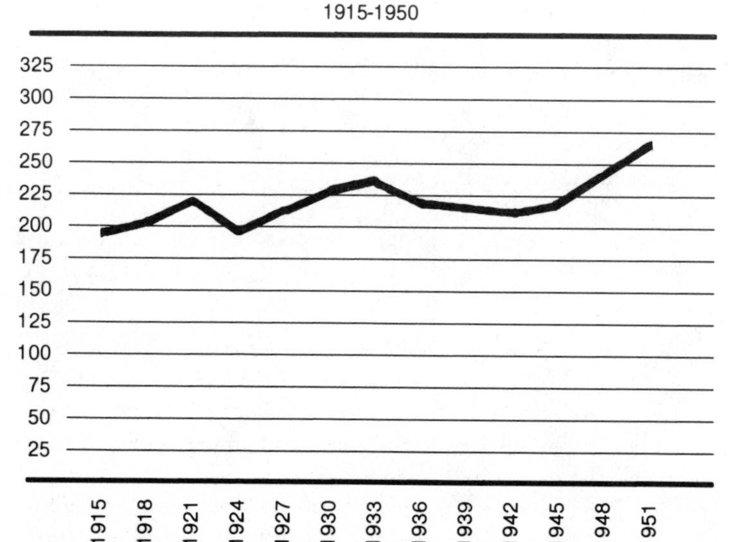

*Now let's visit a Sunday School in 1981 . . .*

Sunday morning and you have just finished a delicious breakfast of eggs ($1.15 a dozen), bacon ($1.63 a pound), and milk ($1.25 a half gallon), which was purchased at the local supermarket. The headlines of the paper read, "Nuclear Reactor Malfunctions."

As you drive to church from your home in the suburbs, there is no music, because of the noise pollution ordinance. You study the gas gauge in your car apprehensively, for energy is an ever-increasing problem. Because almost everyone drives to church, usually from 5 to 15 miles away, finding a parking place is difficult in the church's facilities.

Overall Sunday School attendance is down when compared to the "good old days." The drop has been especially noticeable in the last 15 to 20 years. A number of the declining classes have merged, so fewer classes are available. Attendance has continued to decline, however, even in the merged classes. The idea of starting new classes has not been mentioned for some time, since it is felt there is plenty of room for newcomers in the existing classes. Replacing teachers is a troublesome problem which seems to arise more frequently.

People in the immediate neighborhood seldom come to church or show any interest in the Sunday School. The neighbors are different from most present members, and little effort is being made to reach out to them. The only contact with people of the immediate area, in fact, is at Christmas when presents are distributed.

It became fashionable some years ago for Sunday Schools to have a bus ministry, and three buses are now parked behind the church. However, climbing costs, personnel problems, failure to hold the bused children, and inability to win their parents are causing leaders to question the value of the buses as an effective tool to combat decline. The church is now looking for ways to dispose of them. This is difficult, however, because across the country many other church buses are for sale.

Small groups that meet in homes during the week for Bible study have become popular; some feel, at the expense of Sunday School enrollment. A few members, subconsciously, are wondering whether the Sunday School may now be outdated. Others have quietly discussed how some churches are experimenting with restructuring the Sunday School hour. Some feel that changing the name to "Bible study hour" might help.

If you listen carefully you may hear, in one of the children's departments, the singing of "Onward Christian Soldiers," but most of the children don't know that song.

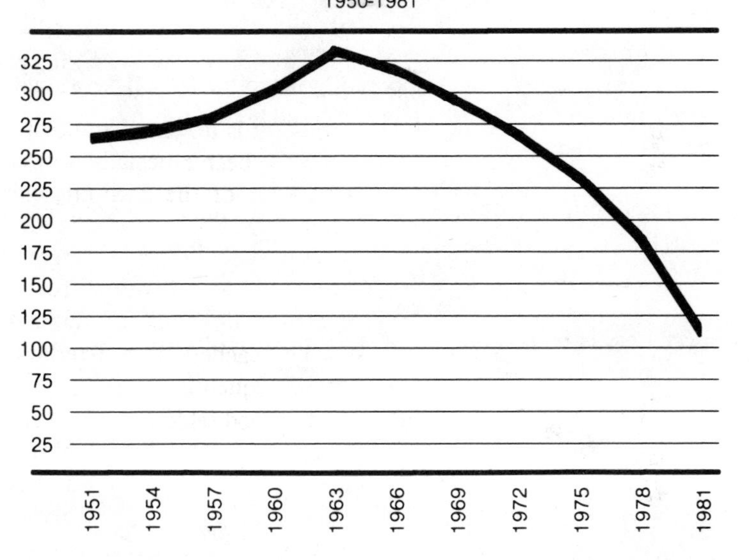


The third part of this century, of course, is not yet completed; much is still to be written about the Sunday School. However, changes in the Sunday School are most evident. Here are a few which have occurred.

## FROM YESTERDAY TO TODAY

*1. The focus of the Sunday School changed* from those "outside" to those "inside." Sunday School conventions, teacher training programs, curriculum material all began to focus attention on the "how's" of teaching, while the "why's" of teaching became more obscure.[1] The result was a decreasing interest in outreach and an increasing interest in nurture. The Sunday School fell prey to the tendency of many institutions to change from the founding goals to goals of organizational survival.[2] Internal concerns became a preoccupation, capsizing the delicate balance of ministry *to* the body and ministry *through* the body.

2. *Leadership of the Sunday School shifted* from the laity to professionals. Age-grading encouraged specialization.[3] There was less involvement by the many, and more involvement by the few. The Sunday School, which was once totally administered by laity, was now only partially administered by laity. The Christian Education Director emerged as a new vocation which lifted much of the responsibility from the laity. Lay people were no longer the generals in the Sunday School, but became the foot soldiers.

3. *A separation of roles evolved* in the Sunday School and church. The *evangelist* became the zealous, pulpit-pounding, uncompromising charismatic leader whose message was to "repent and be saved." Evangelism was what *he* did during a special crusade in a church or a downtown auditorium. When the crusade was finished, so was evangelism—until the next crusade.[4]

The *religious educator* became the thoughtful, quiet planner whose message was "let us grow spiritually." His concern was spiritual nurture, and he primarily focused on present church members and their children. Bringing Christians to spiritual maturity was his major objective. Consequently, he had little time or concern for evangelism.

The *laity* became those who participated in activities planned for them. They filled the chairs and watched the events. Except to serve on committees, usually focused on internal concerns of the church, roles of the laity were passive.

These roles and expectations became more distinct and separated as the century progressed.

4. *There developed a loss of community and sense of belonging.* The neighborhood church changed to a "drive-in" church. Members saw each other only on Sundays. Young people had other friends during the week. Adults lived in two worlds—Sunday and the rest of the week. Because of this, person-to-

person relationships became less meaningful, resulting in the decline of a caring fellowship.

The growing ease with which people could travel outside their immediate neighborhood, brought a decline in the sense of "community" with the people in the immediate neighborhood. The feeling of community, which once came naturally into the Sunday School as an extension of neighborhood life during the week, was not actively nurtured when the community concepts began to change. As the years passed, the Sunday School seldom acted deliberately to meet this new challenge, and the meaningful relationships, which once characterized the Sunday School and the church, grew fewer and fewer.

*5. The Sunday School became less and less of a priority* for the church. At one time, the Sunday School was an exciting adventure which demanded and received a top priority of the laity. There were large Sunday School conventions to attend. There were weekly training classes. Sunday School attendance and offerings were recorded on a sign at the front of the sanctuary. Attendance awards were given. But as other tasks became important, the Sunday School was less and less perceived as a top priority for the church.

You as reader, from your own experience, could probably add other changes that took place in the Sunday School. The changes, of course, did not happen in every church or denomination at the same time, or with the same degree of intensity. Yet, they do provide a valuable perspective to the recent history of today's Sunday Schools and Church Schools. Indeed, these developments have important implications for the future of our Sunday Schools today.

## THE LARGER PICTURE

Such historic glimpses of one particular Sunday School might be only interesting or nostalgic reading, except for one thing—they closely reflect what has occurred in a great many Sunday Schools across the nation.

During the first and second thirds of the twentieth century, American churches and Sunday Schools skyrocketed in unprecedented numerical growth.[5] Downtown "First Churches" flourished. As both rural and urban churches began to grow, new Sunday Schools were established at a record pace. Large Sunday School conventions were held and Christian educators were in great demand. Sunday School growth seemed to happen with little or no effort. The "Golden Age of American Sunday Schools" had arrived. Churches, too, enjoyed vigorous growth.

But as the century moved into the late 60's, while few noticed, growth patterns began to change. In many Sunday Schools, enrollment began to plateau. Attendance stabilized or started a slight decline. Church membership followed. The decline didn't happen to every Sunday School or denomination at once. Nor was there a "Black Sunday" that educators recall as the turning point. But the tide had turned. The "Great Depression" of the growth of many American Sunday Schools and churches had begun.

At first, church leaders saw the plateau as a chance to consolidate their numbers and make "better Christians." As the decline steepened, rationalizations appeared. By the time church and Christian education leaders faced the significant changes

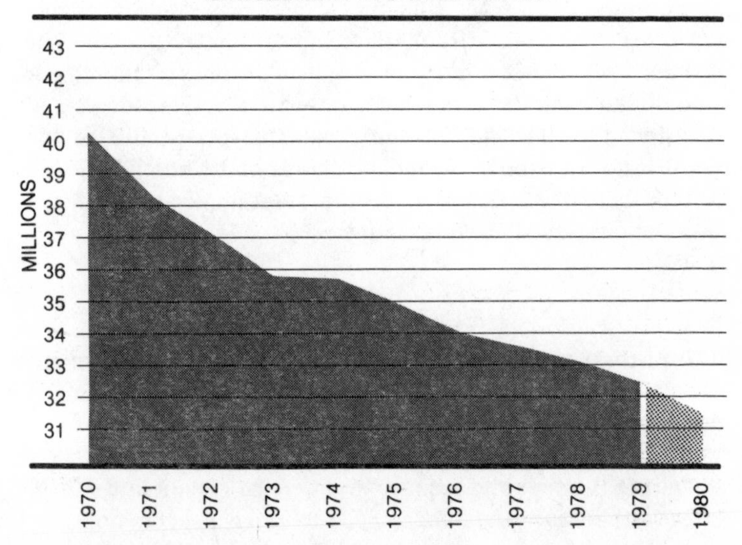

that were actually taking place, many Sunday Schools and entire denominations were in an accelerating tailspin. And few workable solutions were forthcoming.

Traditional seminary courses did not deal with evangelism and church growth. Religious educators in training had no experience with reversing such a decline. Local church and Sunday School leaders were faced with problems for which they had no answers . . . many did not even agree on the questions.

The decline of the Sunday School continued into the '70s. Mainline and evangelical Sunday Schools alike found the cancer of decline difficult to arrest. In 1974, national Sunday School enrollment dipped, for the first time in history, below its expected growth rate based purely on national population trends. In fact, if the decline in national Sunday School enrollment continues at the rate it has since 1970, in two generations the Sunday School, as we know it, will become extinct! Today, at the outset of the 1980s, after nearly 200 years as a growing institution, the Sunday School is in serious trouble.

Total Sunday School, Church School, and Sabbath School enrollment in American churches has declined from 40,508,568 in 1970 to 32,607,421, a 24% decadal decline! This decline, moreover, has occurred in spite of an increasing trend in church growth. Total church membership, during this same period, grew more than 16%. But *in nearly every major Protestant denomination, Sunday School/Church School enrollment is now rapidly declining.*[6]

Of 42 major Protestant denominations in America, 24 reported at least some growth in confirmed membership in 1980. Of that same 42, however, only nine registered any growth in their Sunday School, only three of these grew over 1%, and only one denomination has shown a *consistent* pattern of growth in recent years.[7]

Between 1960 and 1966 seven of the largest Protestant denominations in the United States[8] reported their highest Sunday School enrollment ever.[9] From this peak in the mid-60s to the present, however, all of these denominations have experienced substantial declines in Sunday School or Church School enrollment. Research also indicates that in *every* Protestant denomination, Sunday School, as a proportion of total church membership, is steadily declining.[10]

## MAINLINE SUNDAY SCHOOL DECLINE

Mainline congregations and denominations, over the last decade, have taken a beating in Sunday School/Church School enrollment.

The *Lutheran Church, Missouri Synod* has declined from 885,567 enrollment in 1969 to 638,074 . . . a 28% loss; compared to approximately 1% gain in church membership during the same period.

The *United Presbyterian Church in the USA,* since 1970, has lost over 30% of its enrollment.

*American Baptist* Church School enrollment has dropped from 651,054 in 1969 to 437,937 in eleven years . . . 32%.

The *Episcopal Church* has declined from a peak enrollment of over 980,000 to their present 574,693—a 41% loss.

In 10 years, the *Christian Church (Disciples of Christ)* has lost 302,780—more than 45% of its enrollment.

The rate of church school enrollment growth in the *United Methodist Church* exceeded U.S. population growth until 1964.[11] But since its peak, the church has lost 2,524,365 from its Church Schools.

In overview, while mainline church membership has been dropping in recent years, Church School enrollment is declining at a substantially greater rate.

## EVANGELICAL SUNDAY SCHOOL DECLINE

The cancer of decline in Sunday School enrollment does not stop with mainline denominations, but includes many classified as "evangelical." For example, the *Christian and Missionary Alliance* has grown nearly 40% since 1970. Sunday School enrollment has dropped 8%.

The *Church of the Nazarene* has grown 33% since 1965, and has shown steady church membership growth each year since. In the last year reported, however, the denomination lost 24,441 in Sunday School. The year before that, Sunday School enrollment declined by 28,429.

The *Assemblies of God* have grown 64% in church membership since 1965. Enrollment growth in Sunday School, however, has grown 33%, or approximately one half.

The *Free Methodist Church,* growing at a ten year rate of 16%, is declining 6% in Sunday School enrollment.

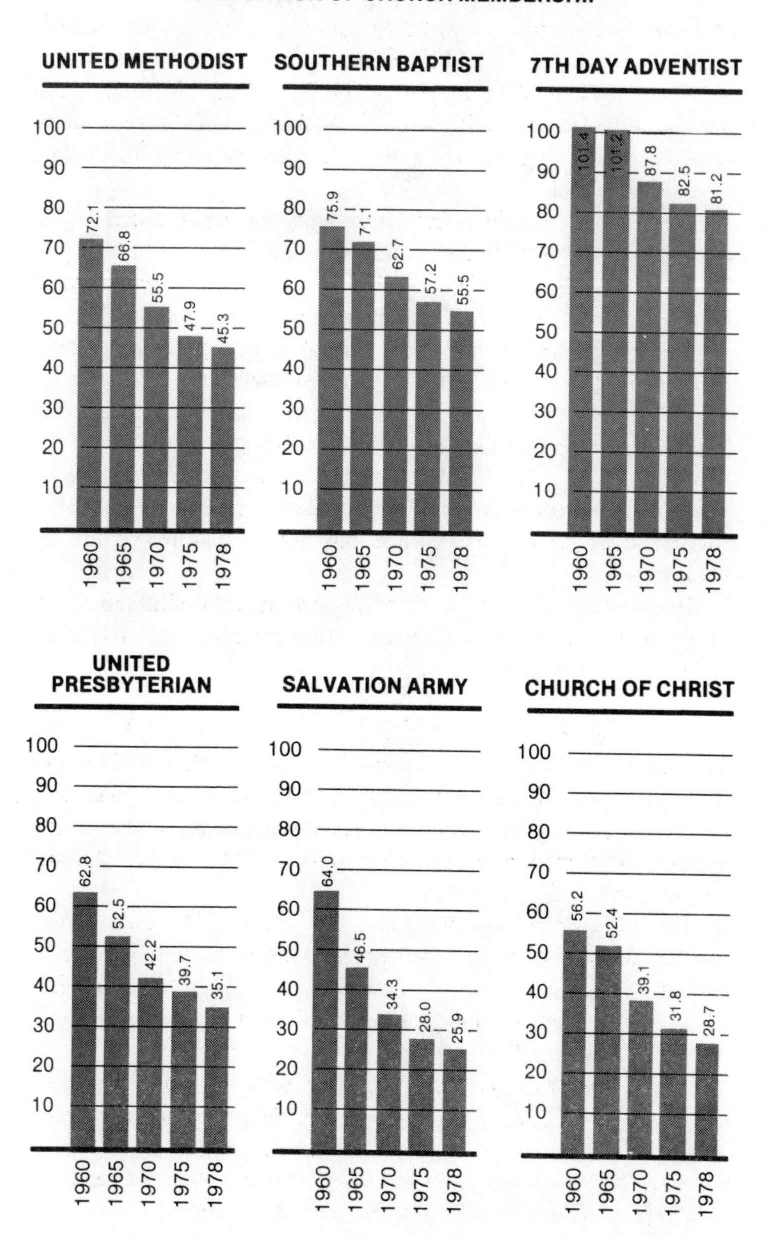
SUNDAY SCHOOL AND CHURCH SCHOOL AS PROPORTION OF CHURCH MEMBERSHIP
UNITED METHODIST
72.1
66.8
55.5
47.9
45.3
SOUTHERN BAPTIST
75.9
71.1
62.7
57.2
55.5
7TH DAY ADVENTIST
101.4
101.2
87.8
82.5
81.2
UNITED PRESBYTERIAN
62.8
52.5
42.2
39.7
35.1
SALVATION ARMY
64.0
46.5
34.3
28.0
25.9
CHURCH OF CHRIST
56.2
52.4
39.1
31.8
28.7
100
90
80
70
60
50
40
30
20
10
1960
1965
1970
1975
1978

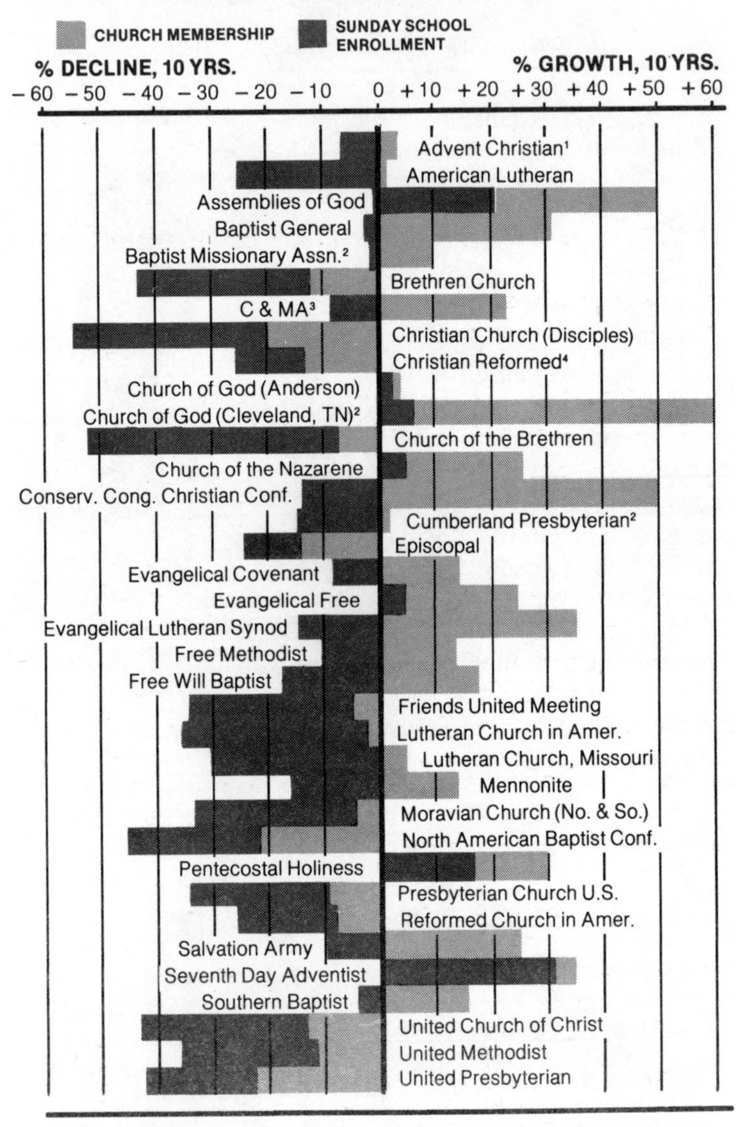


*Source: 1970 and 1980 *Yearbook of American and Canadian Churches,* unless otherwise noted.

1. From 1972 and 1980 Yearbooks
2. From 1971 and 1980 Yearbooks
3. From 1972 and 1979 Yearbooks
4. From 1971 and 1979 Yearbooks

The *Mennonite Church,* in the last 10 years, has grown from 85,343 to 97,142—13%. Yet in the same period it has declined more than 14% in Sunday School enrollment.

Even the huge *Southern Baptist Convention,* which places so much emphasis on the Sunday School, in the four most recent years reported, has lost over 140,000.

Similar patterns of church membership growth, together with Sunday School enrollment decline, are occurring in the *Baptist General Conference, the Wesleyan Church, Salvation Army, Evangelical Covenant Church, Church of God (Anderson), Mennonite Brethren, Advent Christian,* and most other "growing" evangelical denominations.[12]

This unmistakable decline of the Sunday School, in both mainline and evangelical bodies, is also reflected in the shrinking number of Americans being exposed to Christian education. Research indicates that in 1952, 6% of those surveyed had received no religious training as a child. In 1965, that percentage had grown to 9%. In 1978, 17% indicated they had received no religious training.[13]

Indeed, the prognosis for the Sunday School, that once great and thriving institution of the American church, may be rapidly approaching "terminal." The question must be asked, "Is there really a future for the Sunday School?" As the nation moves toward relativism and secularism . . . as the Christian education of children, youth, and adults continues to decline, is there any hope?

## FOOTNOTES

### CHAPTER TWO

1. Carl Combs, "Building a Growing Sunday School," VINELIFE (March 1979), p. 15.
2. Lyle E. Schaller, *Hey, That's Our Church!* (Nashville: Abingdon, 1975), p. 125.
3. Judy Meyers, "Is Your Sunday School Ready for the 80's?" THE STANDARD 70, no. 1 (January, 1980), p. 3.
4. Research indicates that the farther evangelism is from the activities of the local church and the laity in the church, the less effective it will be in showing responsible church membership as a result. For two excellent research studies on the "mortality rate" of mass evangelism when measured in terms of responsible church members, see "Mass Evangelism: The Bottom Line" CHURCH GROWTH: AMERICA (January/February, 1978) 4, no. 1;

and "A Church Growth Look at Here's Life, America" CHURCH GROWTH: AMERICA (January/February, 1977) 3, no. 1.

5. Dean R. Hoge and David A. Roosen, eds. *Understanding Church Growth and Decline,* 1950-1978. (New York: Pilgrim Press 1979), p. 17.
6. All figures, unless noted otherwise, are taken from the various editions, up through 1980, of the *Yearbook of American and Canadian Churches,* Constant H. Jacquet, ed. (Nashville: Abingdon).
7. Seventh Day Adventists have consistently averaged 3-5% growth in their Sabbath Schools. In 1978 they grew from 428,251 to 477,208 (11%). Since 1970 they have grown from 369,212 (29%).
8. Southern Baptist Convention, United Methodist Church, United Presbyterian Church in the U.S.A., The Episcopal Church, Lutheran Church in America, Lutheran Church (Missouri Synod), the American Lutheran Church.
9. Ruth T. Doyle and Sheila M. Kelley, "Comparison of Trends in Ten Denominations 1950-1975" in *Understanding Church Growth and Decline 1950-1978,* ed., Dean R. Hoge and David A. Roosen (New York: Pilgrim Press, 1979), p. 154.
10. Calculated using previous editions of the *Yearbook of American and Canadian Churches.*
11. Warren Hartman, *A Study of the Church School in the United Methodist Church* (Nashville: Board of Education, 1972), p. 5.
12. It is startling to realize that among the few denominations where Sunday School and church membership are both growing, there are no denominations where Sunday School enrollment is growing at the same rate as or a greater rate than membership. In every denomination where Sunday School and church membership are both declining, Sunday School enrollment is declining at a more rapid rate than church membership. And while there are numerous denominations where church membership is growing and Sunday School enrollment is declining, there are no denominations where Sunday School enrollment is growing and church membership is declining. On the whole, the Sunday School appears to be in a much more precarious position, concerning growth, than church membership in every denomination in the country.
13. George Gallup, "The Unchurched American," CHURCH GROWTH: AMERICA 5, no. 2 (March/April, 1979) p. 9.

# GROWTH: IMPORTANT FOUNDATIONS

YES! There is hope for the Sunday School!

Despite the sobering statistics on national Sunday School trends, there is hope. The first light of a new dawn can be discerned. There *are* growing Sunday Schools; in fact, some are bursting at the seams. In every denomination and every part of the country there are education programs for children, youth, and adults that are enlisting new members and growing with explosive vitality. Some Sunday Schools are reaching, winning, and discipling new people into active fellowship of local churches. Today, while some Sunday Schools are fading into oblivion, others are teeming with contagious vitality.

Why?

Why do some Sunday Schools burst with life, while others shrivel and die? Can it be, as many believe, that the quality of teachers makes all the difference in a growing Sunday School?[1] Or do growing Sunday Schools require several dozen buses and pandemonious quarterly attendance contests?[2] Can Sunday School classes that provide meaningful Christian growth and maturity become contagious and turn enrollment decline into active new growth?

Insights on why *churches* grow or decline have been rapidly emerging from the new field of study called "Church Growth." During the 1970s considerable research and attention were focused on the decline of church membership which plagued many American denominations. As denominational executives and local pastors began learning and applying church growth theory, substantial new membership growth has been, and continues to be, realized. The insights developed through the church growth movement, and disseminated by such organizations as the Institute for American Church Growth (Pasadena, CA), have been greatly used by God for the growth of His church. Increasing numbers of churches are discovering this fresh breeze of hope and new life as they apply the insights and principles of church growth.

But what of the Sunday School? Research by the Institute for American Church Growth indicates that a growing church does not, by any means, insure a growing Sunday School. While many congregations, and even entire denominations, are realizing substantial membership growth, their Sunday Schools and Church Schools continue to decline. Indeed, the figures from the previous chapter vividly indicate the peril that continues to face the Sunday School.

Insights from the church growth movement have not before been systematically focused on the current problems of the Sunday School. The remainder of this book, however, is an important first look at some of the principles of church growth that do relate directly to the Sunday School and must be applied there. The Sunday School does *not* have to decline: there is hope.

## WHAT IS THE GOAL?

Growth is best understood as it relates to a goal. *Growth,* by definition, means progress toward a goal. A goal provides the target and a way to measure progress.

D. Campbell Wyckoff, nearly twenty years ago, stated the simple implication of goals and priorities facing the Sunday School:

> All education clearly implies a process toward an end. The end, the goal, gives it direction. Purpose, to a large degree, determines what shall be included in the educational process, what shall be stressed, and what shall be played down or omitted.[3]

It is therefore important to confront the question, "What is the goal of Christian education?" The response to this question, to a very large extent, determines the potential growth available to a Sunday School.

A common goal of Christian education is often stated something like this quotation from the eminent authorities Sanner and Harper:

> The objective of Christian Education is to help persons to be aware of God's self-disclosure and redeeming/seeking love in Jesus Christ, and to respond in faith and love—to the end that they may know who they are and what their human situation means, grow as sons of God rooted in the Christian community, live in the Spirit of God in every relationship, fulfill their common discipleship in the world, and abide in the Christian hope.[4]

What is wrong with this impressive-sounding definition? It seems to cover all the necessary basics. Or does it?

Many definitions of Christian education are seriously warped if they are made before considering a more fundamental question—"*What is the purpose of the church,* of which Christian education is a support agent?"

However, even this is not the first question which must be asked. If we believe the church to be the Body of Christ, the Household of God, and if we see the church existing in this world to do the will and accomplish the purpose of God, we need to ask: "What is *God's* will and purpose for His people and His church?"

Scripture bears clear testimony: God's unswerving purpose is that lost mankind be redeemed and brought into His church. Christ's birth, crucifixion, and resurrection were for the purpose that mankind might be saved.

Christ opened a way of salvation so that all people, everywhere, might find forgiveness of sin, reconciliation to God, new life in Christ, and become members of His Body—the Church. This primary purpose of God, proclaimed by Christ's disciples, is the motivation and power behind growing churches.

That God purposes the redemption of lost mankind is the testimony of Scripture in its entirety. One can hardly open the New Testament without encountering this truth. Passage after passage clearly underscores God's will that all come to a knowledge of the truth. Not all will come. Some, alas, will reject His love. But the Bible tells us that He does not wish *any* to perish. Jesus testified that He came specifically to seek and to save the lost. The Book of Acts is the record of how those in the early church, in obedience to God's will, aligned themselves with this unswerving purpose; and the Church grew.[5]

Perhaps the clearest statement of God's purpose is found in Christ's final words to His disciples, recorded in Matthew 28:19-20: "Go, then, to all people everywhere and make them my disciples, baptizing them in the name of the Father, the Son and the Holy Spirit, and teaching them to obey everything I have commanded you . . ."

The Greek verb forms used in Matthew 28:19-20 give us insights into the Lord's desire for His church. The only *imperative*

**A SEVEN-MINUTE INTRODUCTORY BIBLE STUDY**

God's unswerving purpose in sending Jesus Christ to earth is recorded throughout the New Testament and appears time and time again. In this brief and introductory study, look up the following Scriptures. Write down the main theme of each verse.

1. Luke 19:10 ____________________
2. II Peter 3:9 ____________________
3. John 3:15 ____________________
4. I Timothy 2:1-4 ____________________

What other verses reflect the purpose of Christ's coming to earth? (Luke 15:7; John 3:16; John 15:8, etc.)

____________________

Jesus states succinctly in Matthew 16:18, ". . . I will build my ____________, ____________

____________________."

verb in Christ's command is "make disciples." There are *helping* verbs: "going," "teaching," "baptizing," but all these amplify the goal of making disciples.

So, the purpose and priority of God is clear. What does this mean for the church—Christ's Body on earth? What does it mean for the Sunday School—the major teaching organization of that Body?

## MISSION-ORIENTED

Christ's life was mission-centered. He was *sent* by the Father (Mark 10:45). His marching orders to the church make it abundantly clear that He conceived of the church as mission-oriented (Matthew 28:19-20). "As the Father sent me, so send I you." Being Christ's church, therefore, requires commitment—above

Christ's concern for *building His church* is well documented and established. Look up and read the verses below which shed light on how and through whom Christ builds His church:

NOTES

1. Romans 10:13-15 ______________________
2. John 20:21 ______________________
3. Acts 1:7-8 ______________________
4. Matthew 28:19-20 ______________________
5. John 15:16 ______________________
6. Mark 16:15 ______________________
7. Luke 24:47-48 ______________________
8. Luke 10:1-13 ______________________

The early disciples knew the importance of growth and recorded their awareness often in the book of Acts. Look up the following verses in the book of Acts:

| | | | | | |
|---|---|---|---|---|---|
| 1:15 | 2:41 | 2:47 | 4:4 | 5:14 | 6:1 |
| 6:7 | 9:31 | 11:21 | 16:5 | 21:20 | |

all else—to Christ's own mission in the world.

Christian educators concerned with being true to Christ's desire for His church, are inevitably faced with the question, "Is the purpose and nature of our Christian Education/Sunday School program accurately reflecting the mission of Christ and His church?"

This question must be asked and answered by leaders in the local Sunday School and Christian education program. Aligning the Sunday School's purpose with His is *the* crucial issue. This objective cannot be treated as another item on the list of educational objectives. It is not an additional purpose clause to be added. This is *the* most important question which the Sunday School must face—and resolve—before it can fulfill its rightful purpose.

Perhaps the major difference between Sunday Schools that are growing and Sunday Schools that are not growing is in their view of purpose. Whether specifically stated, or subtly implied, every Sunday School and church has a "philosophy of ministry"—a reason for existence. *The "purpose for being" is nearly always different in declining Sunday Schools than in growing ones.*

## INWARD-FOCUSED SUNDAY SCHOOLS

In most declining Sunday Schools the "reason for being" is exclusively ministry to existing Christians and nuture to members of existing churches.

While a concern for the spiritual health, the personal growth, and the social fellowship of Christians within existing Sunday Schools is necessary, in declining Sunday Schools these concerns have become the entire preoccupation of the classes and curriculum.

What happens when the priority of Christian education focuses exclusively on nuture of existing Christians? People are urged to participate in the Sunday School because it will help *them.* The church is thought of as a refuge for intimate fellowship with other believers; a personal and spiritual center where *believers* are nurtured to spiritual maturity. Programs, activities, and curricula are focused almost exclusively on the personal concerns of existing Christians.

An example of the curriculum emphasis of an inward-focused Sunday School can be seen in the following statement of purpose:

> The United Church Curriculum centers in these Christian tasks, which are all part of one pilgrimage of faith . . . 1) to grow in relation to God; 2) to develop trustful and responsible relationships with others; and 3) to become a whole person.[6]

There is nothing *wrong* with these important tasks. They are *parts* of the total emphasis. But in inward-focused Sunday Schools, they become the *whole* emphasis.

The activities in inward-focused Sunday Schools also reflect an introverted concern toward their own members. Social activities are member-oriented with little or no effort to find and bring in non-Christians. Visitors often have difficulty crossing "barriers" of existing social relationships or exclusive tradition. Growth, if it occurs at all, happens almost entirely because of *transfer* growth of existing Christians. A closer look at some of the "fastest growing Sunday Schools" in fact, will show that such transfer growth accounts for much of their increase.

Growth of inward-focused Sunday Schools, through reaching unchurched people in the community, is either not mentioned or is assumed to be an automatic by-product of nurture. Larry Richards verbalizes such a view in *A Theology of Christian Education:*

> As the first concern of the church we must retain the nurture of the Body. For this is God's strategy . . . as we grow into His likeness, His love will motivate us, His concern energize us, and the evidence of His presence enable us to witness in power.[7]

Would that this were true! Unfortunately, the belief that Sunday School growth will naturally result from personal growth and spiritual development of existing members is one of the primary reasons many Sunday Schools today are declining. Such self-centered education *does not* motivate people toward involvement in the church's mission of growth and outreach.[8] Education that concerns itself with only the spiritual nourishment of its own members, contributes significantly to a "self-service mentality" that effectively seals off the Sunday School from the outside world.[9]

Below are the minutes of a teachers and staff meeting held in an inward-focused Sunday School. Can you identify the most important concerns of the members?

1. The meeting was opened with prayer by the pastor.
2. Under "Old Business," a report on the Mariners' class social was presented by Assistant Pastor Anderson. He reported an excellent time was had by all, and that there was 100% attendance by all members.
3. Superintendent Hawkins reported that in the last quarter, a total of 85 new people visited the Sunday School classes. The question was raised concerning the number of visitors who have since become members. Mr. Hawkins said he believed that there were several, but he was not sure.
4. Under "New Business," a motion was presented by Mrs. Green of the adult department to limit to existing members certain classes that were using a continuous quarterly curriculum. The reason for the motion was that visitors seem to impede the progress of the class, since they must be "brought up to speed." The motion was seconded and passed.
5. A motion was made by Mrs. Hallwyler to merge the two junior high classes beginning next quarter. Teachers and aids were reported hard to find, and there was enough room for both groups to meet together. The motion carried.
6. Mr. Bornkamp moved that a new class be started in the senior adult department with the particular aim of reaching single senior adults. He felt that there were different needs among this group and there might be better opportunity to reach new people with a second group. Opposing arguments were presented that suggested there was plenty of room in the existing class

for new people, and that no such request had been heard from any single senior citizens. The motion was deferred.

7. A motion was made by the superintendent that next week a special Sunday School-wide offering be taken to provide money to repaint and carpet the Maranatha Women's classroom. The motion carried.

8. Mrs. Johnson moved that a sub-committee be formed to graph various records and trends concerning Sunday School attendance during the past year. Superintendent Hawkins mentioned that he was quite sure the statistics were not reliable, even if they could be found. He thought the project would probably involve an expenditure of $300 to do it right, and said there was no such money available. The motion was defeated.

9. Curriculum for the next quarter of adult Sunday School electives was presented by the planning sub-committee. The subjects were as follows:
   a) Deeper spiritual life study
   b) Prayer and meditation
   c) Walking closer to God
   d) Loving one another

   The topics were unanimously approved.

10. Mr. Peterson, of the high school department, expressed the desire of several of the high schoolers to become involved in helping neighbors clean up around their yards from the recent storm. The consensus seemed to be that it was an excellent idea. The suggestion was made that these young people concentrate particularly on helping neighbors who were presently members of the church.

11. The meeting was adjourned by the pastor.

*Respectfully submitted,*
*Ester Van Liew*

Dr. Kenneth Van Wyk, director of a growing Christian Education program at Garden Grove Community Church (Garden Grove, CA), underscores this point:

> In my judgement, nurture-oriented education commits the serious error of making an end out of something that is meant to be a means. By definition it is self-centered and therefore suffers from a basic introversion. It violates the example given us in Christ's teaching and life, where ministry on behalf of others is central and primary.[10]

*In most declining Sunday Schools, the programs, curriculum, activities, and training do not reflect the priority of outreach required by Christ for His church.* Further study shows that not only are such inward-focused Sunday Schools a deterrent to growth, they often fail to reach the very goal they do have—to develop greater spiritual maturity and Christ-likeness among existing members. A Sunday School not concerned with or participating in the central purpose of fulfilling Christ's Great Commission is actually stunting its members' spiritual maturity and subverting its goal of developing Christ-likeness.

## OUTWARD-FOCUSED SUNDAY SCHOOLS

The purpose of most *growing* Sunday Schools, on the other hand, is quite different. Outward-focused Sunday Schools exist to obey Christ's Great Commission, and to equip the laity for ministry to the world. While concern for spiritual growth and nurture of existing Christians is a crucial part of all curricula and activities, it is seen as a means to an end, not an end in itself . . .

> Christian Education is missionary education by definition. It is participation in Christ's invitation to join in God's mission to the world . . . God's mission, His purpose and plan for the world, is that He desires all men to be saved and come to the knowledge of the truth. (I Tim. 2:4)[11]

Outward-focused Sunday Schools, in contrast to inward-focused Sunday Schools, see evangelism and education as two sides to the same coin; two tasks to achieve one goal. Carrying out Christ's commission—to reach and disciple lost people—is the motivation for Christian education in most growing Sunday Schools. The noted Christian educator H.W. Bryne observes:

> Evangelism is the chief work of the Sunday School. In fact, Christian Education cannot be Christian unless it is evangelistic. To fail here is to fail in our primary reason for existence.[12]

In an insightful comparison of growing Church Schools with sharply declining ones in the United Methodist Church, Dr. Warren Hartman, Assistant General Secretary for Church School Development, found nearly twice as many lay people in growing Church Schools who saw the Church School as a place for winning persons to Christ.[13]

The Institute for American Church Growth asked more than 280 pastors and executives from various denominations, "What are the reasons for the present decline of the Sunday School?" The most often listed reason was: "Classes not concerned with reaching/recruiting new people."[14]

In outward-focused Sunday Schools, each class and each department gives high priority to seeking, reaching, teaching, and discipling men and women, boys and girls.[15] The focus of the entire organization, events, classes, curriculum, and activities of growth-centered outward-focused Sunday Schools is toward one goal: *making disciples.* And the result is growth . . . God gives the increase!

## GROWTH—THE NEW VISION

It would be a mistake to conclude that in order to turn a Sunday School around from decline to growth, a concern for spiritual nurture and personal growth must be abandoned or even de-emphasized in pursuit of a "mission emphasis."

Christ did not abandon His disciples after they agreed to follow Him. He spent much time and effort teaching them and encouraging them in their new life. He was, indeed, providing a living lesson of the need for teaching and the necessity of building strong, mature disciples. The spiritual growth and maturity of Christ's disciples were essential if He was to carry out His goal.

Yet, Christ's goal was to enroll disciples. "Follow me" was His command. He did not try to develop a "class of spiritual giants."[16] The training and teaching of His disciples was a means to an end—preparing them to be effective in reaching and winning others. The Book of Acts is replete with accounts of

**Below are the minutes of a recent teachers and staff meeting of an "outward-focused" Sunday School. What are the differences between this meeting and the previous one?**

1. The meeting was opened with prayer by the pastor.
2. Under "Old Business," a report was presented by Assistant Pastor Russell of the Mariners class social. He reported that an excellent time was had by all, and that 17 new people were brought to the event. The class has already begun befriending these new people. All have been invited to the coming Bible study and will be picked up by existing members.
3. Superintendent Rollins reported that in the last quarter a total of 149 new people visited the Sunday School classes. He also mentioned that 47 of these people are now attending regularly as a result of the recruitment effort by individual classes.
4. Under "New Business" a motion was presented by Mrs. Ross of the adult department to open all the classes to visitors. Several adult classes presently discourage visitors since it was once believed that they would inhibit progress. The motion was seconded and passed.
5. A motion was made by Mrs. Benjamin to form a third junior high class this quarter. She mentioned that every time they had started a new class, attendance had grown. The motion was carried and a sub-committee was appointed to begin searching for a teacher and a room in which to meet.
6. Mr. Sutter moved that a new class be started in the senior adult department with the particular aim of reaching single senior adults. He felt that there were different needs among this group of singles and there might be better opportunity to reach new people with a second group. The motion was passed.

7. A motion was made by the superintendent that next week a special Sunday School-wide offering be taken to provide money to purchase copies of *Growth: A New Vision for the Sunday School,* a new book on how church growth principles can be applied to the Sunday School. A copy would be given to each teacher. The motion carried.
8. Mrs. Harris moved that a sub-committee be formed to graph various records and trends concerning Sunday School attendance during the past year. Superintendent Rollins mentioned that he would be happy to work with the committee in securing necessary data and providing any help possible. It was determined that $300 would be necessary to do the research and prepare the important data. The motion was passed.
9. The curriculum for the next quarter of adult Sunday School electives was presented by the planning sub-committee. The subjects were as follows:
   a) How to identify and reach new people
   b) The growth patterns and strategy of the early church
   c) Jesus' parables concerning finding the lost, and their meaning today
   d) Loving and winning our world for Christ's sake

   The topics were unanimously approved.
10. Mr. Jones, of the high school department, expressed the desire of several of the high schoolers to help neighbors clean up around their yards from the recent storm. The consensus seemed to be that it was an excellent idea. The suggestion was made that these young people concentrate particularly on helping neighbors who were not presently members of the church.
11. The meeting was adjourned with prayer by the pastor.

*Respectfully submitted,*
*Mabel Richards*

the growth of the early church and the central role of Christ's "students" in building the church.

The difference between an inward-focused and an outward-focused Sunday School, and in most cases a declining Sunday School and a growing one, is clear. One sees spiritual maturity as an end in itself. The other also sees maturity as an essential part of Christian education, but not, in itself, the end. Rather, spiritual growth of existing Christians is the supporting foundation for redemptive outreach. The goal is making disciples.

The time has come for a new vision of the Sunday School . . . to see the Sunday School through "church growth eyes." What this means, above all else, is to see clearly *the supreme purpose* to which we are called. The past is a rich heritage. The future can be equally as bright. Let us, in obedience to Christ's command, be about our Father's business of *making disciples.*

**WHY SUNDAY SCHOOL?**

1. The Sunday School is a great means of outreach to friends and relatives of existing members.
2. The Sunday School provides the opportunity for establishing and developing personal relationships, which in turn, greatly help in the incorporation of new members into the life of the church.
3. The Sunday School provides a unique opportunity to gain Bible knowledge and to study the applications of the Christian life in today's world.
4. The Sunday School can create new classes which appeal to a variety of new people.
5. The Sunday School provides a system by which the church can minister to entire families. It can include every age group in the surrounding community.
6. The Sunday School is the most natural organization to train and equip large numbers of laity.

## FOOTNOTES

### CHAPTER THREE

1. A study by Warren J. Hartman—*A Study of the Church School in the United Methodist Church* (Nashville: Board of education, 1972) p. 21—indicated that "capable and well-trained teachers" were seen as the major factor which contributed to the growth of the church school by 76% of the pastors surveyed, 86% of the district superintendents, and 60% of the laity.
2. See Elmer Towns *The Successful Sunday School Teacher's Guidebook* (Carol Stream, Illinois: Creation House, 1976), p. 155 and p. 229.
3. Campbell Wyckoff, *Theory and Design of Christian Education* (Philadelphia: Westminster Press, 1961), p. 22.
4. Elmer Sanner and A.F. Harper, *Exploring Christian Education* (Kansas City: Beacon Hill Press, 1978), p. 23.
5. For a complete treatment of this concept, see Donald A. McGavran and Winfield C. Arn, *Ten Steps for Church Growth* (New York: Harper & Row, 1977), chapters 2 and 3; and Donald McGavran *Understanding Church Growth* (Grand Rapids: Eerdmans, 1980, 2nd edition), chapter 2.
6. Roger L. Shinn, *The Education Mission of the Church* (Boston: United Church Press, 1962), pp. 66-67.
7. Lawrence O. Richards, *A Theology of Christian Education* (Grand Rapids: Zondervan, 1975), p. 56.
8. David R. Hunter, *Christian Education as Engagement* (New York: Seabury 1974), pp. 72-75.
9. Reginald M. McDonough, *The Minister of Education as a Growth Agent* (Nashville: Convention Press, 1978), p. 9.
10. Kenneth Van Wyk, "Educate for Church Growth" CHURCH GROWTH: AMERICA (March/April, 1978), 4, no. 2, p. 8.
11. Letty M. Russel, *Christian Education as Mission* (Philadelphia: Westminster Press, 1967), p. 38.
12. H.W. Bryne, *Christian Education for the Local Church* (Grand Rapids: Zondervan, 1975), p. 56.
13. Warren J. Hartman, *A Study of the Church School in the United Methodist Church* (Nashville: Board of Education, 1972), p. 20.
14. "Why is the Sunday School Declining?" CHURCH GROWTH: AMERICA (March/April, 1980), 6, no. 2, p. 3.
15. Even within the present enrollment of many Sunday Schools there are prospects for receiving Christ. A Southern Baptist study indicated that evangelistic prospects totaled "about 25% of the enrollment" in most Sunday Schools. R. Othal Feather, *Outreach Evangelism Through the Sunday School* (Nashville: Convention Press, 1972), p. x.
16. Bob Girard, "Jesus Models Discipling," INTERCHANGE (Fall, 1979), p. 3.

CHAPTER FOUR

# GROWTH: MEASURING THE SUNDAY SCHOOL

Helen Randle had agreed to teach a newly-formed class of 10 to 15 young couples. She was petrified! What would she do? How would she prepare? What if the class didn't like what she taught or how she taught it? What if they asked questions she couldn't answer?

She decided it would be good to have a chat with the Sunday School superintendent, just to be sure she wasn't getting herself or the church into something both would later regret.

Harold Brown, a teacher himself for nearly 15 years, was reassuring when they met for lunch to discuss Helen's apprehensions. "What worries me the most," Helen reflected, "is that I may be just wasting their time when they could be really learning and growing."

"Helen, tell me why you think we have a Sunday School," the superintendent inquired.

"Well, to build up Christians in their faith. To learn more about the Bible . . . how to live better Christian lives."

"Um hmm. That's right. And why, if you'll excuse my philosophical bent for a moment, do you think we have a church in general . . . with all our groups, activities, worship, Sunday School, and so on?"

"Well, Mr. Brown, I would say really for the same reasons. After all, shouldn't all the groups in the church have the same basic goals as the total church . . . to strengthen Christians, teach them more about the Bible and God's word, help them live better lives for Christ, and develop meaningful relationships with other Christians?"

"Yes, they certainly should. Tell me, Helen, what about reaching people outside of Christ? Do you think that is part of the purpose of the church?"

"Well, certainly. Christ said, 'Go, and make disciples.'"

"And how do you think that task might be carried out, Helen?"

"I suppose by evangelistic things. And when the pastor visits someone in the hospital who doesn't go to church. Or if someone in the church won a friend to Christ, they would probably come to our church."

"Do you remember the first time you brought your friend Marcia to a church function?"

"Of course. In fact, it was the Sunday School picnic. We were all encouraged to bring a friend who didn't regularly go to church."

"That was two years ago. Since then Marcia has become a Christian and an active member of our church and Sunday School."

"And she's brought two of her friends to Christ and our church, too."

"Yes. Isn't that great! You, Helen, and Marcia and her friends, are excellent examples of the philosophy we have tried to develop throughout our Sunday School, and why our Sunday School is one of the few in the area that is growing. Our 'philosophy of ministry' sees the Sunday School not only as an important place to build relationships among Christians, to study the Bible and its relevance to our daily lives, but also as an excellent way to reach out to people not presently in the church and to win them to saving faith in Christ."

"Well, Mr. Brown, it seems like if we spend all our time working on evangelism there's not much time left for spiritual growth or building relationships. I mean, I'm not against evangelism, but can we really do both well?"

"Helen, do you remember when Marcia first accepted Christ?"

"Yes, I certainly do. I had been praying for her for a long time, and when I saw God answer my prayer it was just so thrilling!"

"And then you helped her in her own spiritual growth, through Bible study and prayer with her . . ."

"Yes. And, you know, she's doing the same thing now with her friends that just came into the church."

"Do you recall how you felt when Marcia accepted Christ and then while you were helping her grow in her new faith?"

"To tell you the truth, Mr. Brown, it was one of the most satisfying times of my life. We studied and prayed and learned together. I wish I could do it all over again."

Helen Randle was about to begin a new way of looking at old stereotypes. She would find, in the months ahead, that her new role as a Sunday School teacher would be one of the most satisfying and rewarding adventures of her life. She would learn about the growth of her church, and how the Sunday School, and even her class, played an important part in that growth.

Helen would discover that a Sunday School can do more than strengthen the spiritual lives of the "flock" and teach "our" children in the faith. She would discover that some of the greatest joys and spiritual growing experiences in the Christian life come in reaching out to others and being involved in the process of nurturing new "babes" in Christ.

The Sunday School, in Helen's church, had become an important arm of implementing the philosophy of the entire church—finding, reaching, winning, and discipling men and women. Put simply, the church and Sunday School had developed excellent "growth eyes"—the ability to see the Sunday School as a way to reach and incorporate people into the Body of Christ. A Sunday School with growth eyes sees lost people in its community and is determined to reach those people for Jesus Christ and His Church.

The church where Helen Randle is a teacher has discovered

another very important aspect of what it means to see through growth eyes. The church has realized that successful, growing churches organize every function and activity of the church to contribute to the total goal; every activity must support that goal. So, while there are *many ministries* of the church, there is only *one mission:* to make disciples.

Superintendent Brown, in a later conversation with Helen, likened their own Sunday School to a modern real estate business. Everyone knows, he explained, that a real estate company exists for the purpose of selling houses. All of its people are employed, in some way, around this activity. Some function as secretaries in a supportive role, some research the market, others are salespeople and work with customers. However, the bottom line is whether the company sells houses. If it achieves its goal, the company is successful. If it doesn't, then all the work done by the various departments is to no avail. When houses are not being sold, the company will do well to review its procedures and determine how to sell houses more effectively. If it is discovered that money or time is being spent which does not contribute to the goal, then reallocation is necessary.

The same principle holds true with Sunday School leaders who see through growth eyes. When a Sunday School is properly "employing" its members, they should all be directly or indirectly involved in achieving the church's basic goal. When the Sunday School is actively winning people, making disciples and incorporating them into the Body, it is successful. When it is not, then it declines and the church declines. Success is in doubt. And if it is discovered that money or time is being spent in the Sunday School which does not contribute to the goal of making disciples, a reassessment of priorities should be made. Woman power (and manpower) should be reallocated.

An outward-focused Sunday School not only provides for the spiritual growth of its members, but also makes it a priority to structure programs, groups, and activities toward reaching and discipling people for Jesus Christ. Evaluation of budget and priorities are measured as they relate to fulfilling the goal Christ gave to His church—making disciples. This includes going, baptizing, and teaching . . . for the purpose of making disciples.

## A SECOND VISIT

Let's visit again with our friends, Helen Randle and Harold Brown, several months after their first conversation, as Helen begins to sharpen her own growth eyes. Helen has had a good experience and has gained confidence in herself; she enjoys her new role as a teacher. The Sunday School superintendent has asked her to help with the quarterly analysis of the Sunday School....

"Thanks for agreeing to help the Sunday School planning committee, Helen. We're getting a lot more data than we first expected, and we'd like to put the information in the hands of our teachers as soon as possible."

"I'm certainly glad to help, Mr. Brown. I am also interested in what you are doing with all these charts and graphs. I thought only the church treasurer kept such things."

"Well, all right. You asked for it. But first, let me show you some of the charts we are already keeping on a weekly basis. Here are the weekly attendance charts of every class in the Sunday School."

"Wow! That's interesting. Attendance seems to be going up in some of the classes and down in others."

"Yes. We have found it very helpful to know which classes seem to be reaching, as well as keeping, new people. As you can imagine, if visitors don't come back, then not much is accomplished. These charts tell us how each class is doing in reaching their short- and long-term growth goals."

"As a teacher, I feel like someone is watching over my shoulder, keeping all these graphs."

"Well, don't get too unsettled. After all, we are all on the same team. If there are any facts we find that would be of value to you as a teacher, we want you to know about it. It's something like a football team with assistant coaches watching the plays from the press box above the stadium. If they discover something that would help the team, it's their job to get the information to the coach and players."

"I see . . . I suppose I'm still getting used to the whole idea of teaching."

"You're doing an excellent job, Helen. I've heard nothing but good things about your class."

"Thank you. By the way, what is this line graph?"

"That's the total Sunday School attendance during the past year, week by week."

"It looks like we finished the year with more people than we started with. Although it does seem to go up and down during the year."

"Yes, we find that the attendance varies from month to month. As you can see, the summers are down. The months around Easter are normally high. We keep yearly records and compare them to previous years, which helps us see trends from month to month. But you are right, overall we have seen good growth."

"How much did we grow last year?"

"We grew about 22%. But that figure doesn't tell us very much by itself. We also know that of that 22%, 18% was growth directly traceable to our emphasis on outreach to non-Christians through the Sunday School. About 3% was growth from transfer, and 1% was growth through biological means—members having babies."

"What is this chart? It says 'NEW UNITS.' "

"We keep a close eye not only on total attendance figures, but also on the total number of classes we have in the Sunday School. This graph shows we have added seven classes during the past year, and closed two."

"Our young couples' class must be one of those seven."

"Yes. Which reminds me, I wanted to get your opinion on starting another class for young couples."

"Well, we're certainly happy to have new people join our class. Everyone is very friendly, and I'm sure there's room."

"You know, Helen, we've been studying the growth patterns in our classes, and what we've found seems to validate a good deal of research already done in the area of forming new classes. Two things happen in nearly every Sunday School class. The first is that, while a class may often consider itself 'friendly,' after a time that friendliness is more toward those presently in the class than toward newcomers. And that's to be expected. It's only natural since the group has known each other longer, developed friendships; they feel comfortable with each other. Yet at the same time, newcomers often find it difficult to break in. The second thing we found is that most of our classes reach their maximum growth within six to twelve months. From there on, attendance pretty much reaches a plateau."

"Well, if that is the case, why don't we break up the classes once a year and move them into other groups?"

"We know that wouldn't work. You see, the Sunday School is one of the best ways people in church, and even people outside the church, can find friendship, support, and meaningful personal relationships. We're not trying to break up friendships; we're trying to encourage them. At the same time, the Sunday School has the potential to be very effective in incorporating new members, and new Christians, into the church. It is extremely important to involve newcomers in some kind of role, task, or small fellowship group. We have found that we can provide that opportunity in an excellent way through the Sunday School, and the best way is by starting new classes."

"I've never thought of that, Mr. Brown. I suppose I would feel more a part of a group that I had entered when it was first beginning, rather than trying to join later as a stranger."

"Exactly!"

Helen and Superintendent Brown would spend another half hour reviewing some of the other charts on their Sunday School. Helen would see a breakdown of the different ways in which people had come into their Sunday School in previous years (through conversion, biological growth, and transfer). She would learn that over the past ten years, the Sunday School attendance had been an indicator of Sunday morning worship attendance; when Sunday School attendance increased, the worship attendance increased. If Sunday School enrollment declined, a decline in worship and later membership could also be expected.

"Here's a chart, Helen, that we're particularly interested in keeping current and monitoring."

"Wow! That's a long one!"

"Well, it's so long because we track people over a year's time, and many details need to be noted. It's actually a chart to help us systematically follow the assimilation process of new converts and potential new members into the life of the Sunday School and church."

"Here's Betsy Potter. She is one of the new Christians Marcia led to the Lord. She's in our young married couples' class, along with her husband."

"Right. As you can see here on the chart, the first contact with her by the church was through the ice cream social your class had."

"I remember that. It was about the time we started praying for her to come to know Christ."

"That's right. In fact, here it is on the chart . . . 'Added to class prayer list.'"

"So, someone really does read those cards we have to fill out every week. Look, here's where she and her husband asked Christ into their lives last month."

"As you can see, though, that's not the end of the chart. Actually, it's closer to the beginning. Here we keep track of their regularity of attendance. The pastor has already called on them several times and, as you know, they are presently working through a self-study program for new Christians. Next quarter they will enroll in the new members' class Sunday evening where, among other things, they will learn more about their new faith, and how to share it with their friends."

"You even have a place on this chart for regular checkups."

"Yes. I'm sure you would agree that if we are involved in leading someone to Christ, and then don't concern ourselves with the growth and development of that new Christian, we're committing a serious offense. The fact is, there is at least as much need for prayer, planning, and work to *incorporate* a person into the church as there is to lead him or her to a Christian decision."

"I'm sure you're right. Although I must admit I have seen a decision for Christ as the last step in a process of witnessing and sharing and praying. There really is more, though, isn't there?"

"Yes, much more. Well, we have a few more charts and graphs around. You might want to come in and look through them when you have more time. But let me show you what we're trying to do for the first time this year, and where we need your help."

"I'm happy to do all I can."

"Actually, there are two things that are closely related. First, we presently know the number of unchurched people we have had at least one contact with during the past several years. What we'd like to find out, Helen, is how many new contacts are necessary for every new Sunday School member. If we discover there are four contacts for each new member, then that will be helpful information. If we find there are 18 contacts required for each new member, then that, too, will be valuable to know. You will need to do a little research into these records to see exactly how many people did come into contact with our Sunday School for the first time. Then determine what proportion of these people are now members, regular attenders, or very close to becoming members. You can get the proportion by dividing the smaller number by the larger number."

"That doesn't sound too difficult. That information would also help us predict the number of new contacts we'll need next year to reach our growth goal."

"Exactly, Helen. Now, a second thing. Once we have that general information, we want to analyze it from other viewpoints. For example, does it appear that more contacts are necessary for each new member in the youth department than in the young adult department or singles class? What about the older adults; how many contacts have been made there for the growth we've had? The more data we have, the more we can learn about our strengths, the trends, our growth history and potential."

"I'll get right on it, Mr. Brown, and get back to you as soon as possible."

"Thanks. We're looking forward to sharing this information with our teachers at the next teacher's meeting, so we can begin planning strategy for the next year."

## ABUNDANT INFORMATION NEEDED

There's no doubt that Helen is beginning to understand church growth, and at the same time the leaders of the Sunday School are gathering more information to determine the health of the Body.

Gathering data and analyzing the Sunday School in a variety of different ways is an essential part of understanding how Sunday Schools and churches grow. Compare it to a practice we are all familiar with: when your child is not feeling well, the first thing you probably do is feel his or her forehead for signs of fever. For a more accurate indication, a thermometer will give a better reading. In much the same way, Sunday School leaders should be concerned with monitoring the Sunday School's health. Accurate records are the best way to see present conditions and compare them to past and future projections. While no person has ever been cured by a thermometer, or no Sunday School ever increased just by gathering data, both are essential if remedial alternatives are to be considered and effective measures taken.

Suppose, for example, Helen discovers that 10 new contacts must be made by the Sunday School for every new member. And suppose she finds that only half as many new contacts had been made this year as last year. It would be easier to take remedial action now and consider how to increase the number of contacts than to wait for several years and discover a downward trend in enrollment and wonder why.

Or suppose in other studies it was found that only 2% out of a total Sunday School growth of 22% came through conversion growth, while the other came from biological and transfer growth. It would be obvious that more emphasis should be directed toward reaching unchurched people.

Being conscious of the importance of the growth of the Sunday School is a continuous state of mind. Such people endeavor to see the world from God's perspective: those outside of Christ are lost and God wants them found.

People intent on the growth of the church and Sunday School find out why some efforts of the Sunday School are fruitful, while others are not . . . why some efforts result in growth, while others do not.

Church and Sunday School leaders with growth eyes endeavor to devise bold plans and strategies, under the guidance of the Holy Spirit, which produce actual, factual growth of the church and Sunday School . . . growth which brings people to discipleship and responsible membership . . . growth which is measurable in one year and in five years . . . growth which reproduces itself in new disciples, thereby making better, more just communities.

Look at the graphs, on the following pages, of Helen's Sunday School. They will help you to see how useful the collection and analysis of relevant data can be. How could the accumulation and evaluation of similar data help in your Sunday School?

### RELATIONSHIP BETWEEN SUNDAY SCHOOL AND CHURCH ATTENDANCE

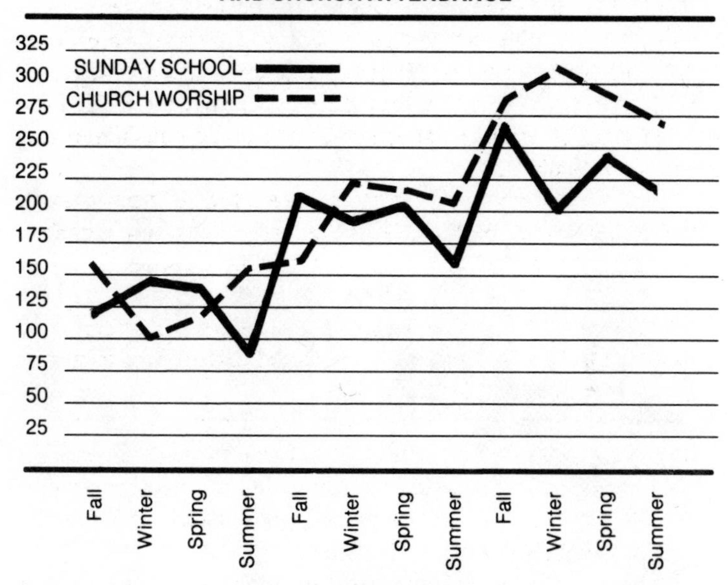


### SUNDAY SCHOOL GROWTH
(BY MONTH)

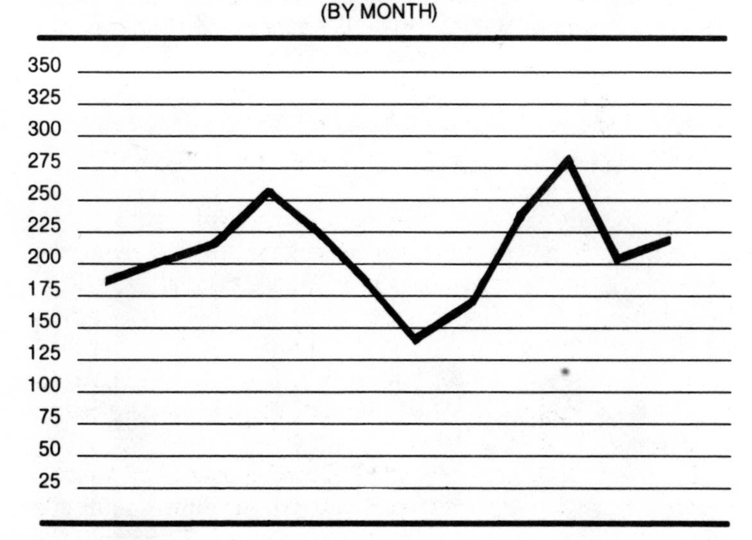

## NUMBER OF ACTIVE SUNDAY SCHOOL CLASSES

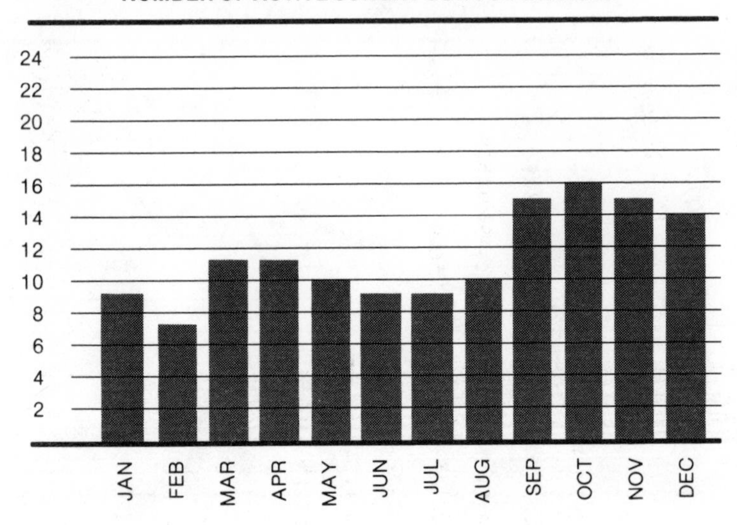


## MEMBERSHIP GAINS AND LOSSES
(PREVIOUS TEN YEARS)

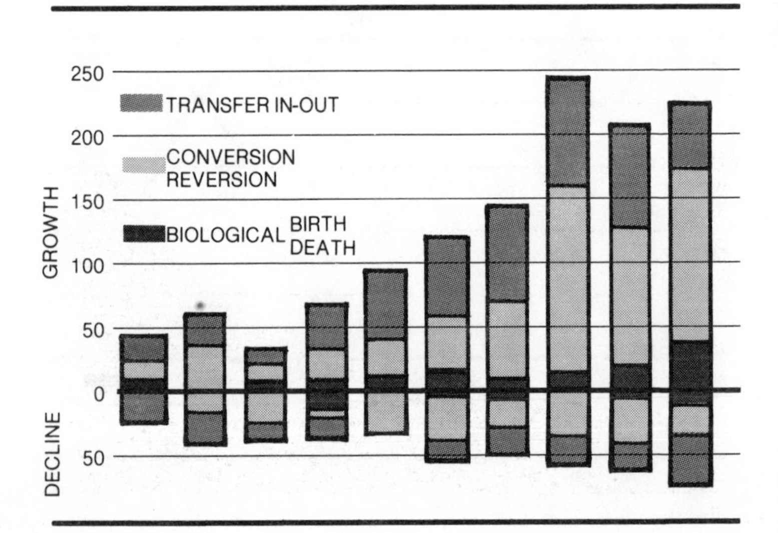

**MEMBERSHIP AGE IN YEARS**

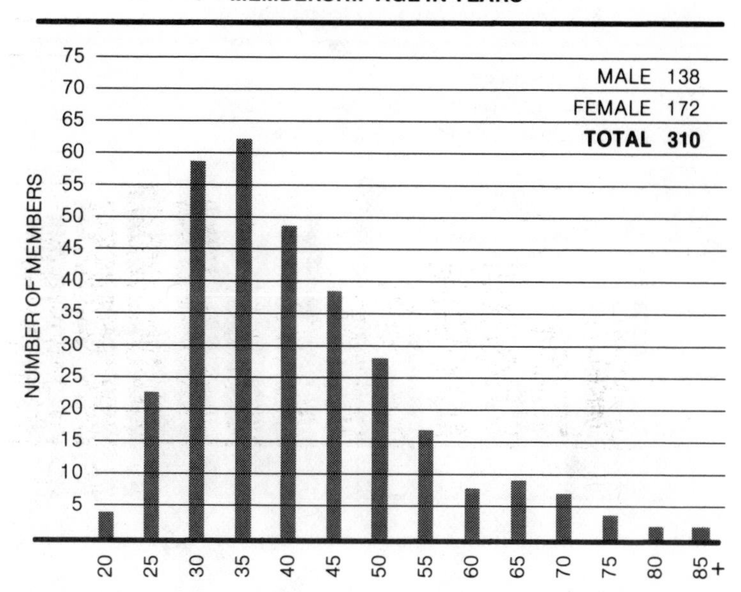


**NET SUNDAY SCHOOL GROWTH**

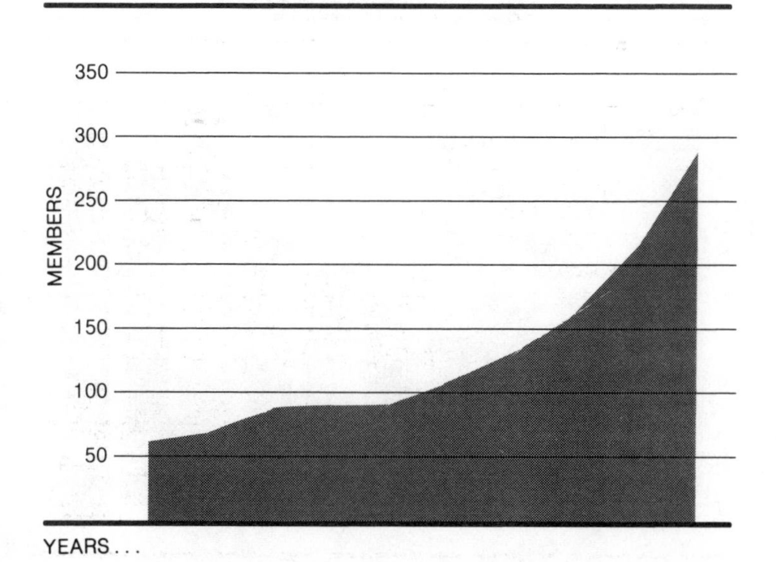

**TOTAL CONTACTS COMPARED TO TOTAL NEW MEMBERS**

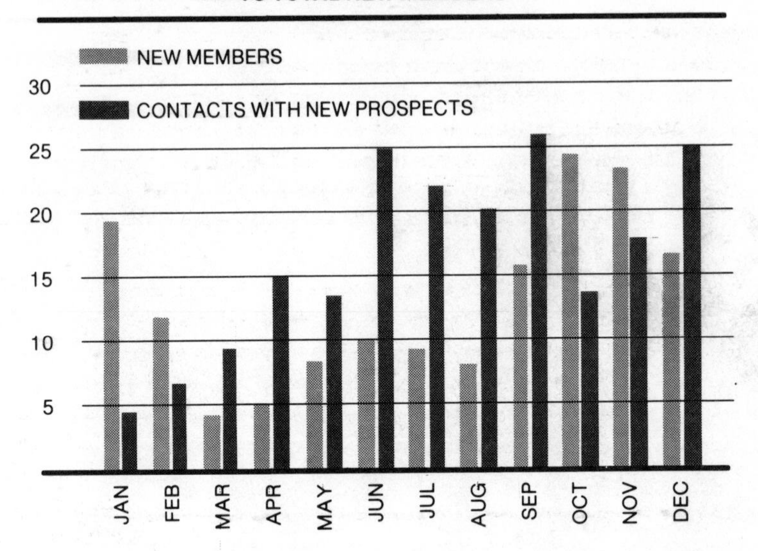


**COLLEGE AND CAREERS**
(ATTENDANCE)

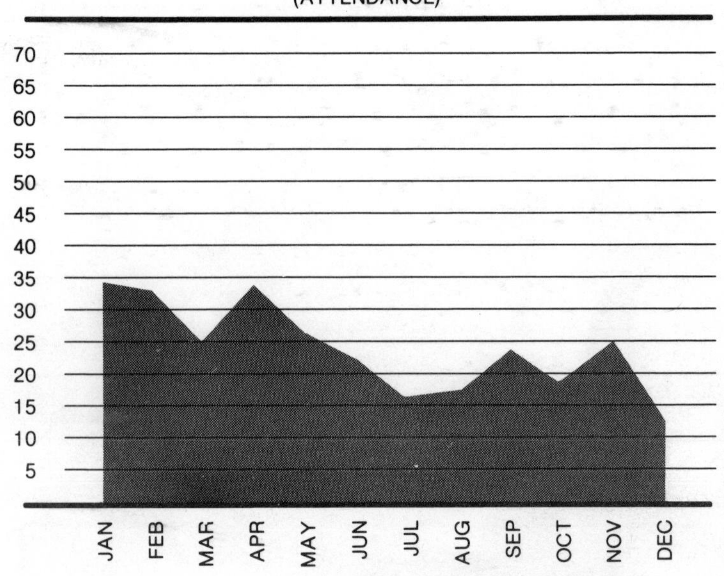

**JUNIOR HIGH SCHOOL**
(ATTENDANCE)

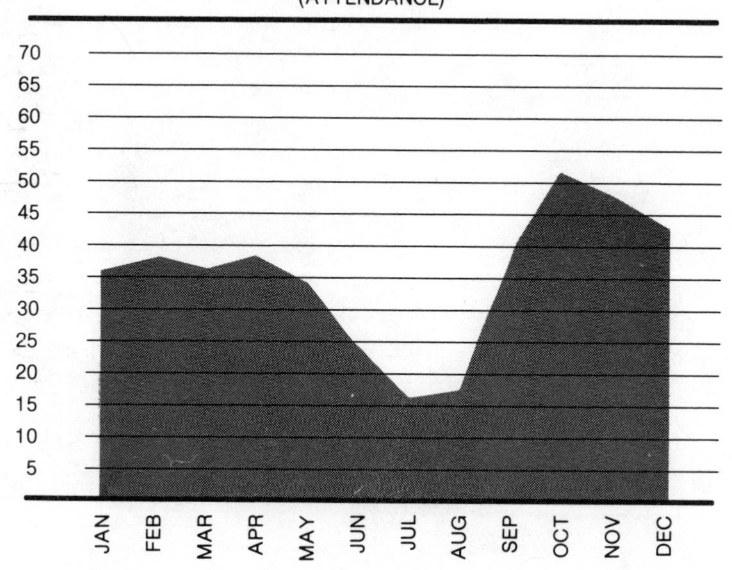


**WOMEN'S CIRCLE #1**
(ATTENDANCE)

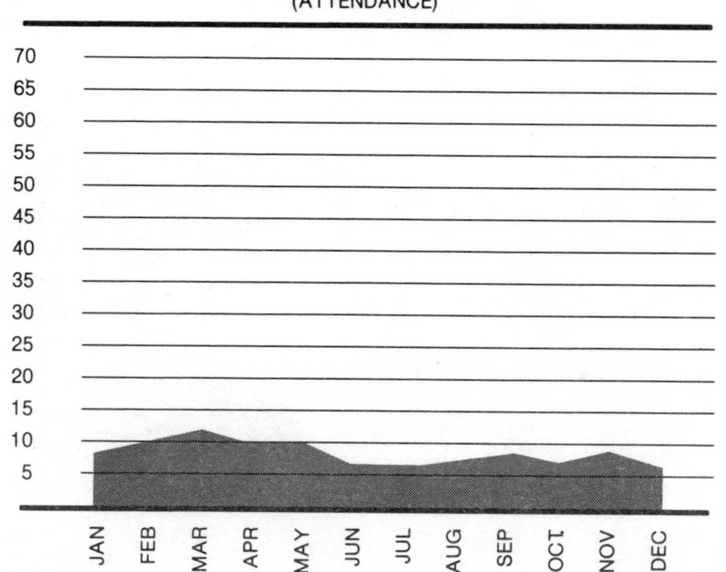

**WOMEN'S CIRCLE #2—BEGAN MARCH**
(ATTENDANCE)

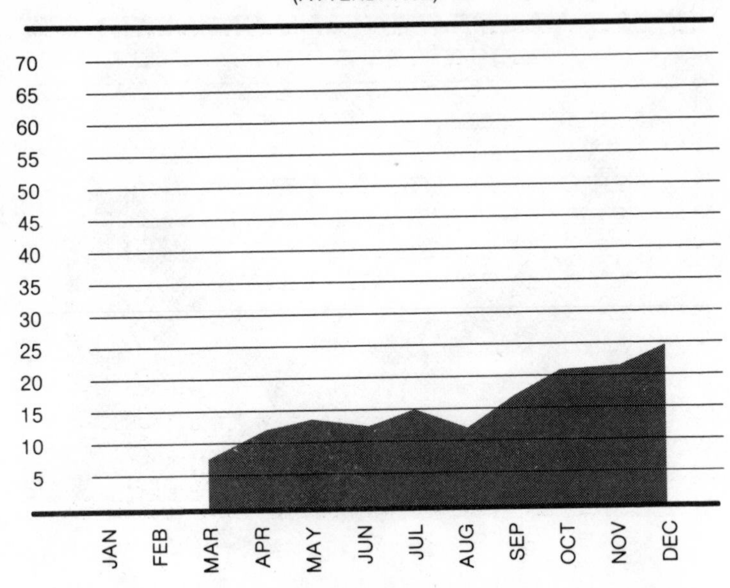


**YOUNG MARRIEDS #1**
(ATTENDANCE)

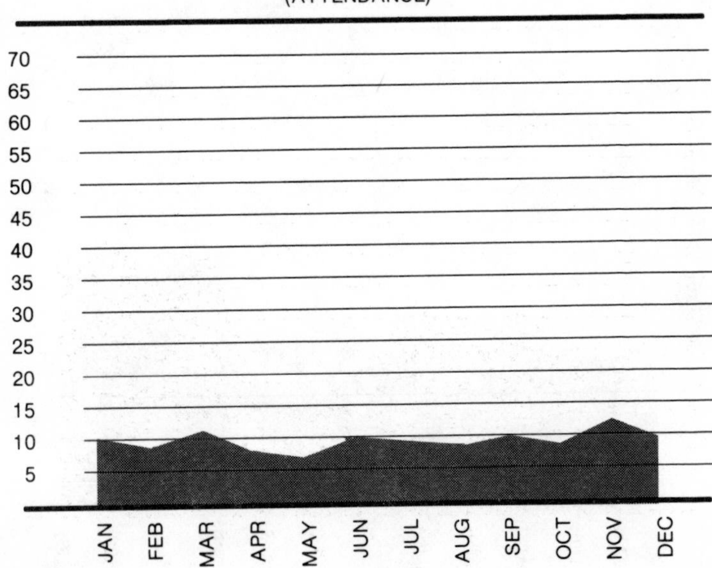

**YOUNG MARRIEDS #2—BEGAN APRIL**
(ATTENDANCE)

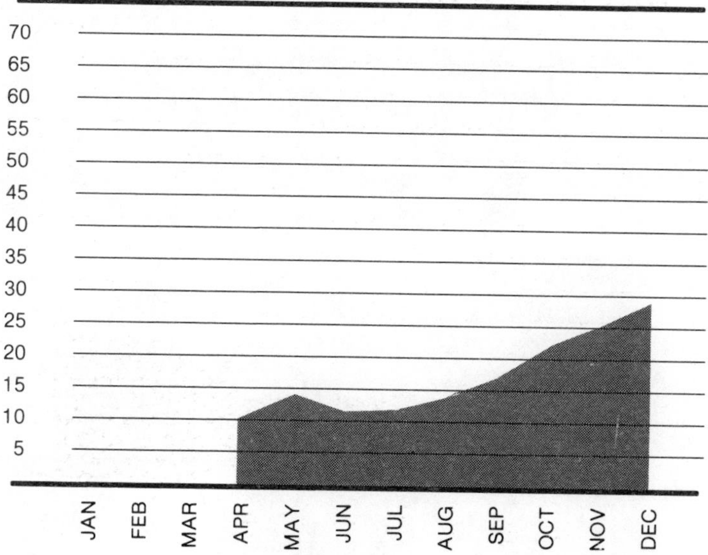


**SINGLES**
(ATTENDANCE)

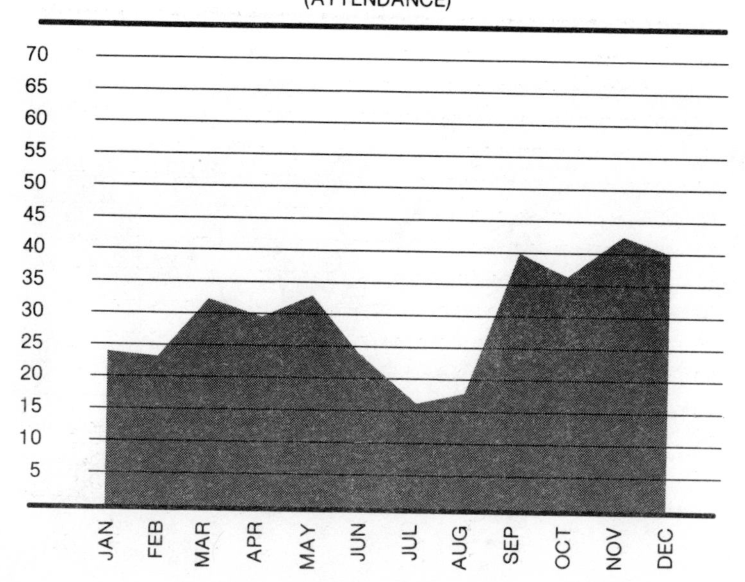

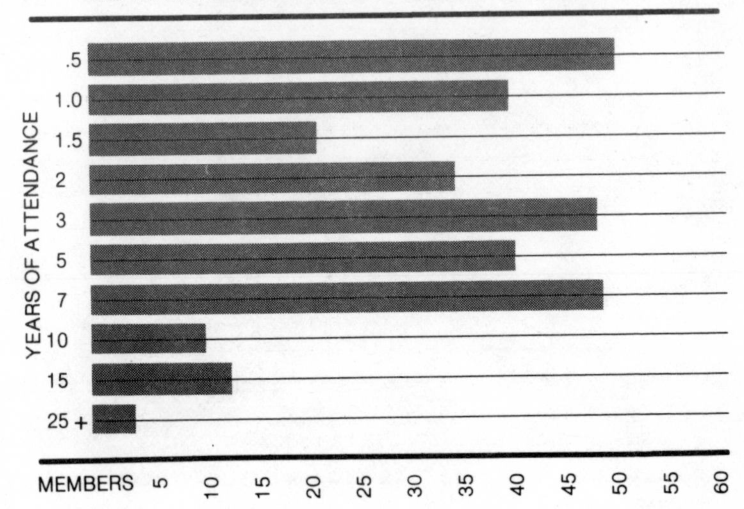
RESULTS OF SUNDAY SCHOOL
MEMBER SURVEY
"HOW LONG HAVE YOU ATTENDED THIS SUNDAY SCHOOL?"
YEARS OF ATTENDANCE
.5
1.0
1.5
2
3
5
7
10
15
25 +
MEMBERS
5
10
15
20
25
30
35
40
45
50
55
60

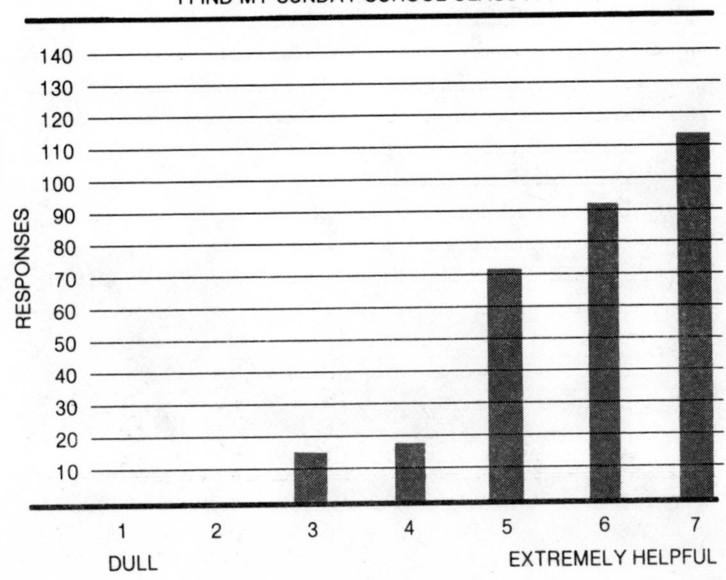
"IN TERMS OF MEETING MY OWN NEEDS,
I FIND MY SUNDAY SCHOOL CLASS . . ."
RESPONSES
140
130
120
110
100
90
80
70
60
50
40
30
20
10
1
2
3
4
5
6
7
DULL
EXTREMELY HELPFUL

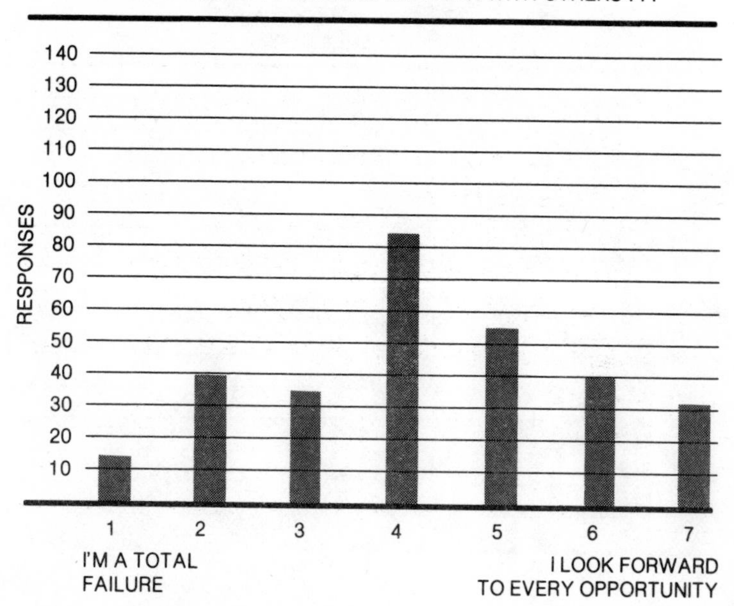
"WHEN IT COMES TO SHARING MY FAITH WITH OTHERS . . ."
140
130
120
110
100
90
80
70
60
50
40
30
20
10
RESPONSES
1
2
3
4
5
6
7
I'M A TOTAL FAILURE
I LOOK FORWARD TO EVERY OPPORTUNITY

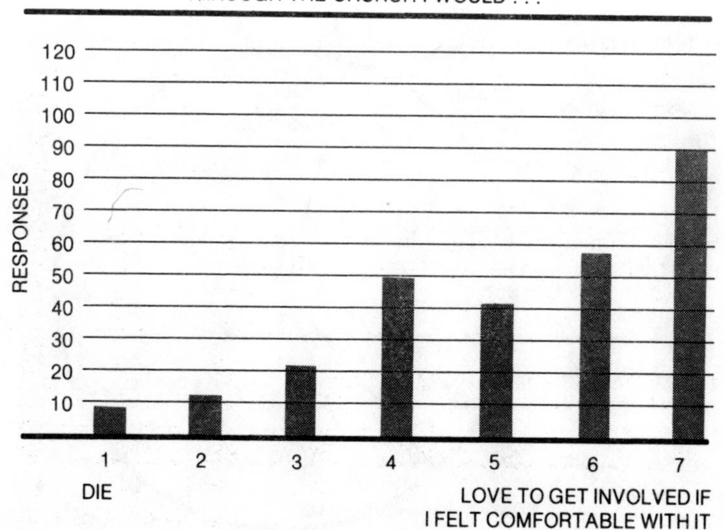
"IF GIVEN THE OPPORTUNITY TO PARTICIPATE IN TRAINING FOR SOME TYPE OF OUTREACH MINISTRY THROUGH THE CHURCH I WOULD . . ."
120
110
100
90
80
70
60
50
40
30
20
10
RESPONSES
1
2
3
4
5
6
7
DIE
LOVE TO GET INVOLVED IF I FELT COMFORTABLE WITH IT

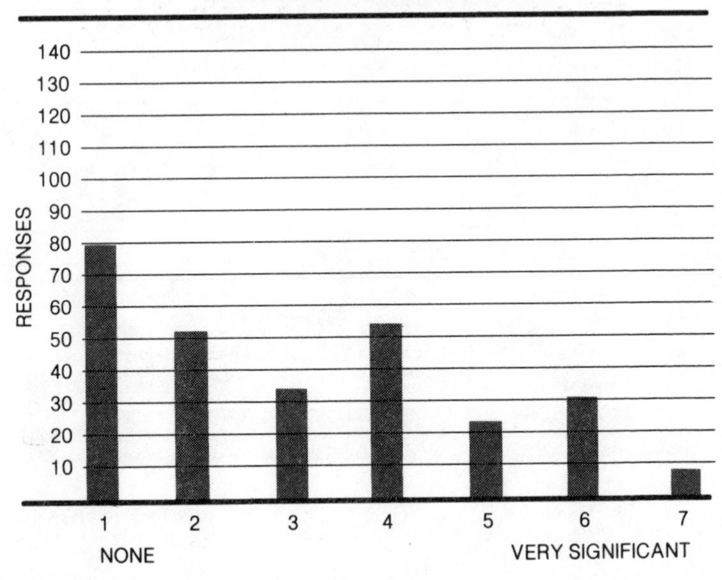
"THE EXTENT TO WHICH I HAVE A PART
IN THE DECISIONS THAT ARE MADE
IN THE SUNDAY SCHOOL IS . . ."
RESPONSES
140
130
120
110
100
90
80
70
60
50
40
30
20
10
1
2
3
4
5
6
7
NONE
VERY SIGNIFICANT

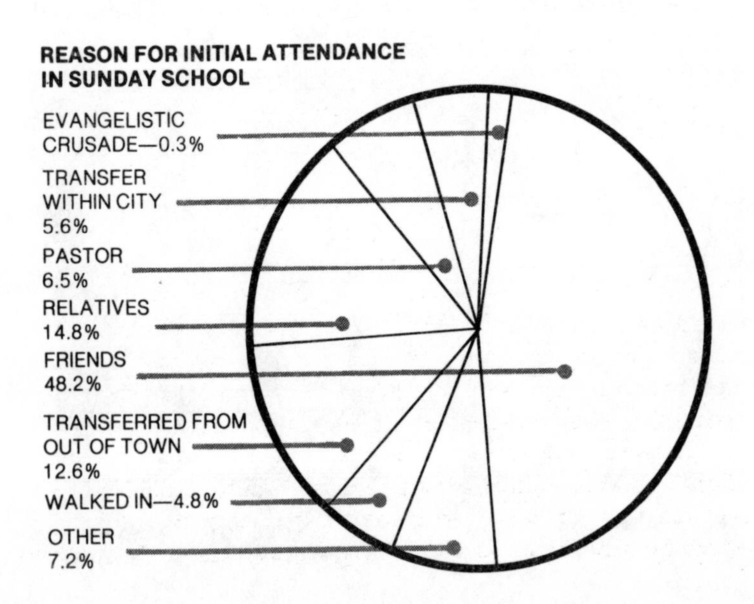
REASON FOR INITIAL ATTENDANCE
IN SUNDAY SCHOOL
EVANGELISTIC
CRUSADE—0.3%
TRANSFER
WITHIN CITY
5.6%
PASTOR
6.5%
RELATIVES
14.8%
FRIENDS
48.2%
TRANSFERRED FROM
OUT OF TOWN
12.6%
WALKED IN—4.8%
OTHER
7.2%

CHAPTER FIVE

# GROWTH: THROUGH OUTREACH

Walk with me through ancient Philippi. Here we will discover timeless growth principles that have thrust churches forward throughout history in exciting, rewarding, fulfilling new growth.

The journey begins as we pull our rented red Volkswagen off to the side of the road and inquire of a Greek farmer the way to a little stream near the ruins of this ancient city. In broken English, and with abundant gestures, he points the way and waves as we drive off.

Philippi, in Paul's day, was a bustling city which Luke describes as "the first of the district, a Roman colony."[1] In 42 B.C. the Roman Republic fought a major battle within sight of the city. To commemorate the victory, the city was renamed Philippensium. The city became a miniature Rome, where Latin was spoken, Roman dress worn, and Roman customs observed. Philippi functioned as a military outpost overlooking the main road tying east and west together. In response to the "Macedonian call," Paul preached his first European sermon in Philippi.

The great apostle was a man of one purpose—to know Christ and to make him known.[2] His method for establishing a new congregation was to visit the synagogue on the Sabbath, where he was invited to speak. His message was of Jesus the

Messiah, of the forgiveness of sins, of freedom from the bondage of law, and of the "power of God for salvation to everyone who has faith, to the Jew first and also to the Greek."[3]

Paul's strategy for growth was to find and win responsive people . . . people whom God had prepared. This strategy meant beginning at the synagogue; then, by following natural webs, to extend the church to its outermost possibilities. In Philippi, however, there was no synagogue. Where would he find responsiveness?

Following the Greek farmer's directions, we turn off on a small, rocky dirt road which turns and twists until the narrowing path comes to an abrupt end.

There we see it!

A small river that circles the ruins of ancient Philippi. Through the centuries, it has etched its way deeper and deeper into the earth. As we trace its turning and twisting bank around the old city, the Scripture, recorded by Luke, vividly comes to mind:

> Here we stayed for some days, and on the Sabbath day we went outside the city gate by the riverside, where we thought there would be a place of prayer, and sat down and talked to the women who gathered there. One of them named Lydia, a dealer in purple fabric from the city of Thyatira, who was a worshipper of God, was listening, and the Lord opened her heart to respond to what Paul said. She was baptized, and her household with her . . ."[4]

Did you see the growth principle? Not only was Lydia baptized, but "her household with her." Paul found receptive people and from there he used the existing "webs" of contacts which these new converts had to their friends and relatives; and from these new converts to other friends and relatives, and to others, and others. A key secret of growth begins to unfold.

We return to the old city and begin exploring the ancient ruins. Pillar by pillar, we walk in the footsteps of Saint Paul. In front of what appears to be a partially reconstructed building, stands a sign—"Paul's Prison." Is this the actual location? No one knows. But the building is not nearly as important as the event itself . . .

> After giving them a severe beating they flung them into prison and ordered the jailer to keep them under close guard.

In view of these orders, he put them in the inner prison and secured their feet in the stocks. About midnight Paul and Silas, at their prayers, were singing praises to God, and the other prisoners were listening, when suddenly there was such a violent earthquake that the foundations of the jail were shaken; all the doors burst open and all the prisoners found their fetters unfastened. The jailer woke up to see the prison doors wide open, and assuming that the prisoners had escaped, he drew his sword intending to kill himself. But Paul shouted 'Do yourself no harm; we are all here.' The jailer called for lights, rushed in and threw himself down before Paul and Silas, trembling with fear. He then escorted them out and said, 'Master, what must I do to be saved?' They said, 'Put your trust in the Lord Jesus, and you shall be saved, you and your household.'[5]

There it is again . . . *webs of growth:* "You and your household." As we study the Scripture in more detail we see that the early church grew primarily through *relationships* between friends, family, servants, neighbors.[6] Indeed, a solid case can be presented that Paul's strategy for establishing churches was, in large part, to find responsive people, convert them, and then reach others in the new converts' webs of relationships. Responsiveness was found as the gospel spread through the webs of family, friends, and associates.

## OIKOS EVANGELISM

The term *'Oikos Evangelism' ("oikos"* being the Greek word for "household") refers to a strategy of identifying existing webs of friends and relatives as the prime source of prospects for Sunday School and church growth.

Examples from the New Testament indicate that *'Oikos Evangelism'* was common as the early faith spread: in Luke 8:39, Christ told the demoniac to return to his *house* and describe the great things that happened to him.

In Luke 19:9, Zacchaeus was told that salvation had come to his *house.*

John 4:52 describes how the centurion's entire *household* believed, following the healing of his son.

In Acts 10, we read how Cornelius, who feared God with all

his *household,* had a vision, sent for Peter, and when Peter arrived, gathered his close friends *(oikos)* together.

In Acts 18:8, Luke describes how Crispus, the leader of the synagogue at Corinth, believed in the Lord with all his *household.*

First Corinthians 1:16 records how Paul baptized the *household* of Stephanas.

In addition to these direct references to the *Oikos* of believers in the rapid spread of the new faith, there are other numerous references where the "web principle" is seen in practice:

Mark 2:14-15 describes how Jesus called Matthew, the tax collector. Soon after, many other tax collectors were dining with Jesus and following him.

Luke 7:37—8:3 recounts how the sinful woman was forgiven, and soon other sinful women were brought to Jesus.

Luke 15 describes the man who found the lost sheep and called his friends and neighbors together to rejoice. In the same parable, Jesus tells of the woman who found the lost coin and brought her friends and neighbors *(oikos)* to rejoice. Finally, the celebration of the son who was found resulted in friends coming together for the joyful reunion.

John 1:40-41 tells of Andrew bringing his brother to Christ.

John 1:44-45 tells of Philip bringing his friend Nathaniel to Christ.[7]

Michael Green, in *Evangelism in the Early Church,* observes that the New Testament church religiously adhered to the strategy of using the household *(oikos)* in the Christian advance.[8] The early Christians knew that when the message of faith was heard and demonstrated by friends and family who were known and trusted, who were "their kind of people," barriers were removed and receptivity to the gospel increased tremendously.[9]

## FAITH DEMONSTRATED

There was a second reason why webs of growth were greatly used by God for the growth of His church. The reason: *faith demonstrated.*

Consider for a moment the Philippian jailer. While the Scripture doesn't record the incidents, can you imagine what remarks were heard among his family, friends, and associates?

WIFE: "You're a different person to live with now; much nicer. I like the new you . . ."

BROTHER-IN-LAW: "I don't know what it is, but the old guy has changed; he's different."

JAILER, FIRST SHIFT: "You should have killed yourself the other night. Why didn't you? And who were those two prisoners you took home to bandage their wounds? That doesn't sound like you."

UNION LEADER: "We're going to have a big party, tonight. Wine, women, song, and prime beef from the temple. Why aren't you coming?"

SISTER: "Let's get the family together so they can all hear about your new faith."

PRISONER: "Could I speak to the jailer . . . the one on duty the night of the earthquake?"

Faith demonstrated—the impact of a transformed life upon those within the web of influence. What is more persuasive to the friends, relatives, work associates of an old friend than a "new" friend? The visible demonstration of the power of God to change lives was at the heart of the growth of the early church—as it is at the heart of the growth of the church and Sunday School today.[10]

## THE IMPORTANCE OF WEBS TODAY

Webs of *common kinship* (the larger family), *common community* (friends, neighbors), and *common interests* (associates, work relationships, recreation) are still the paths most people follow in becoming Christians today. Here are some simple, yet profound, reasons why "Oikos Evangelism" should be a major part in the outreach of any Sunday School:

1. It is the *natural* way churches and Sunday Schools grow.
2. It is the most *cost-effective* way to reach new people.
3. It is the most *fruitful* way to win new people.
4. It provides a constantly *enlarging source of contacts.*
5. It brings the greatest *satisfaction* to members.
6. It results in the most effective *assimilation* of new members.
7. It tends to *win entire families.*
8. It uses *existing relationships.*

Research conducted by the Institute for American Church Growth (Pasadena, CA) on why people first come to Christ and the Church provides astonishing support of the *oikos* strategy of growth and outreach:

Over 10,000 lay people were asked the question, "What was responsible for your coming to Christ and this church?" Usually one of the following eight responses was given: some said a "special need" was the reason; some indicated they "just walked in;" others listed the "pastor;" some said "visitation;" still others mentioned the "Sunday School;" a few listed "evangelistic event, crusade, or television program;" others said the "program" attracted them; finally, some people responded with "friends/relatives."

What percentage of these lay people were in each category? Here are the results of why they are now Christians and members of their church:[11]

| | |
|---|---|
| Special Need | 2% |
| Walk-In | 3% |
| Pastor | 6% |
| Visitation | 1% |
| Sunday School | 5% |
| Evangelistic Crusade | ½ of 1% |
| Program | 3% |
| Friend/Relative | 79% |

Does this enormous percentage of people who come into the church because of a friend or relative (and the comparatively small percentage that come into the church as a result of the Sunday School) mean that the Sunday School should be downplayed as an outreach priority? Not at all. The fact is that a majority of people presently in church came in through the Sunday School.

Do you see the distinction? The *reason* people first come into a new life in Christ and the local church is through the influence of a friend or relative. The *place* of first contact with the church is most often the Sunday School. [12]

Several other research studies shed light on the webs principle of Sunday School and of church growth . . .

One study was conducted a year following "one of the most successful" Billy Graham Crusades ever held in America.[13] What were the results concerning the growth of local churches following the crusade? Questionnaires were sent to 1200 pastors in the greater Seattle/Tacoma area. While a number of interesting discoveries were made,[14] two important insights relate to Oikos Evangelism: 1) Of the total "New Christian" decision cards sent to local churches, only 15% of the people represented were in a local church one year later. 2) However, of that 15% involved in a church after the crusade, 86% had a friend or relative in the church prior to the crusade! Large numbers of these new Christians now in churches were invited to the crusade by friends or relatives. Following their Christian decision, there was a natural "door of entrance" into that same local church.

A second case, which shows the tragic results of what happens when webs of influence are ignored, was the recent mass evangelistic campaign sponsored by Campus Crusade, called "Here's Life, America." This was a huge campaign aimed at saturating metropolitan areas and smaller communities with the Gospel. Millions of dollars were spent on multimedia campaigns using billboards, bumper stickers, newspaper ads, radio and television spots, under the slogan "I Found It!" The campaign was designed, according to its sponsor, to fulfill the Great Commission in America within a matter of years.[15] Churches and laymen were recruited to answer phone calls, deliver booklets, contact people by telephone to explain the "Four Spiritual Laws," and eventually seek a commitment to accept Christ.

A study conducted by CHURCH GROWTH:AMERICA magazine,[16] and later verified by a follow-up study,[17] found that of the hundreds of thousands of decisions registered from the "Here's Life" campaign, *97 out of every 100 were never incorporated into a church!* The campaign, a classic example of "cold turkey" evangelism that ignored existing webs of influence, would have been much more effective and incorporated a much larger percent of its "converts," had it used the principle of webs.

## HOW WEBS WORK TODAY

The Free Methodist Church in Bellingham, Washington, is a typical example of the webs principle of growth in operation. The pastor has kept records of the webs that have been growing in his church and contributing to the outreach of new people. Here is one web that is still growing. It started with a young man named Ron Johnson . . .[18]

**RON JOHNSON**
28 yrs., 5/74

COUSIN

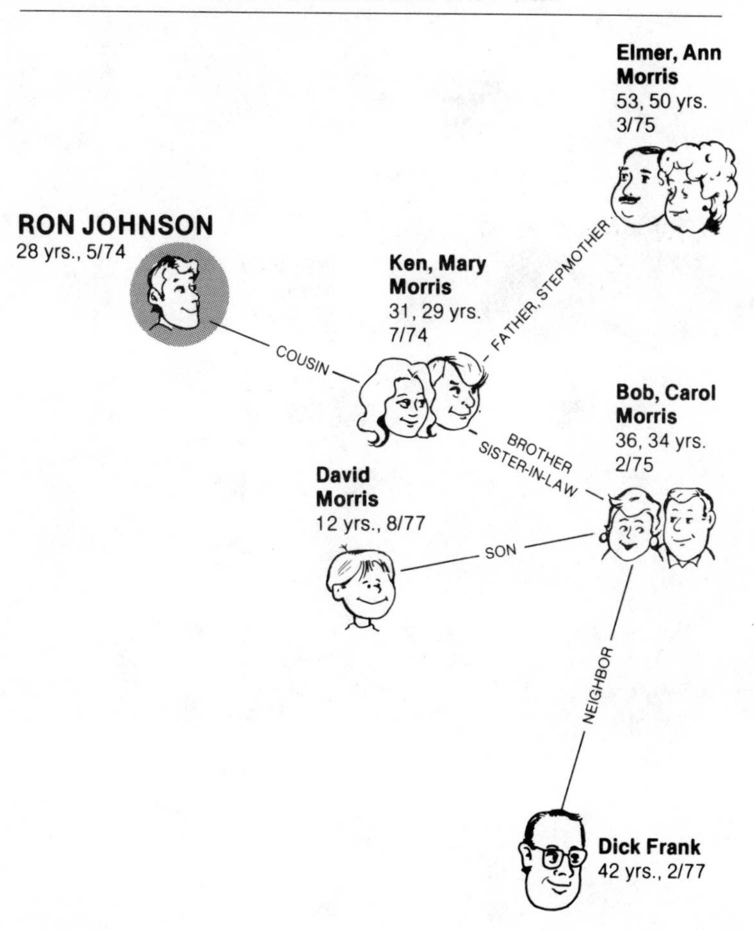
Elmer, Ann
Morris
53, 50 yrs.
3/75
RON JOHNSON
28 yrs., 5/74
Ken, Mary
Morris
31, 29 yrs.
7/74
FATHER, STEPMOTHER
COUSIN
Bob, Carol
Morris
36, 34 yrs.
2/75
BROTHER
SISTER-IN-LAW
David
Morris
12 yrs., 8/77
SON
NEIGHBOR
Dick Frank
42 yrs., 2/77

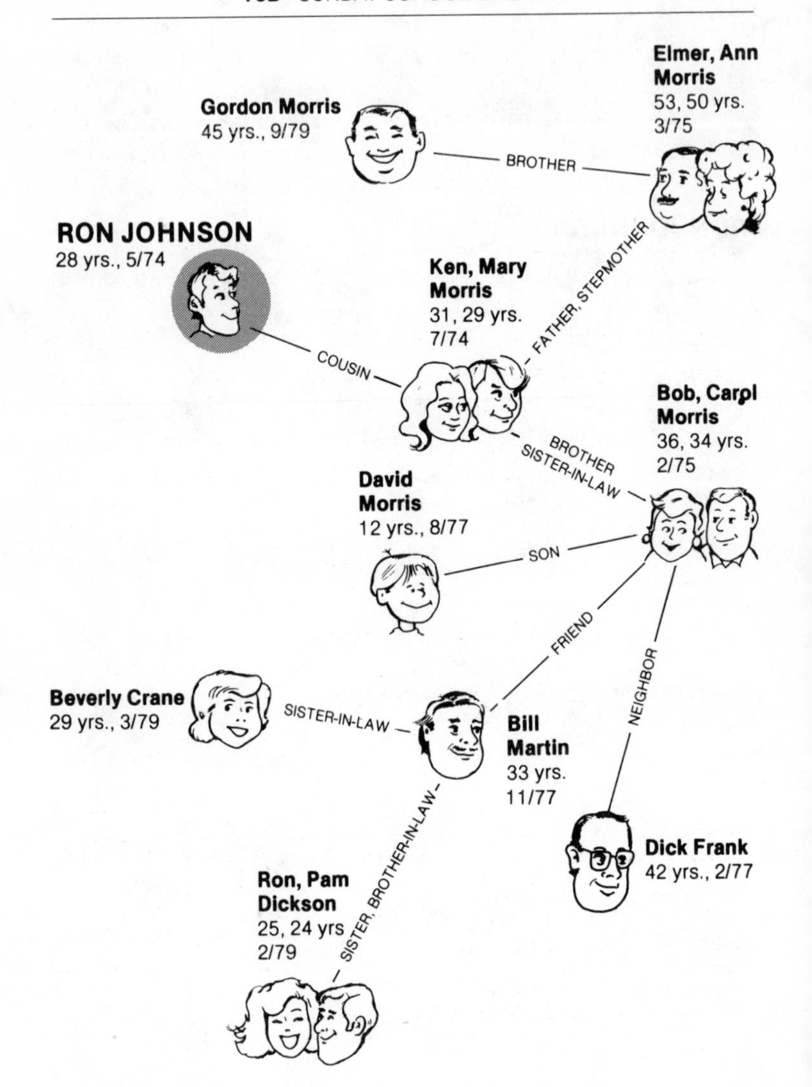
Elmer, Ann Morris
53, 50 yrs.
3/75
Gordon Morris
45 yrs., 9/79
BROTHER
RON JOHNSON
28 yrs., 5/74
Ken, Mary Morris
31, 29 yrs.
7/74
FATHER, STEPMOTHER
COUSIN
Bob, Carol Morris
36, 34 yrs.
2/75
BROTHER
SISTER-IN-LAW
David Morris
12 yrs., 8/77
SON
FRIEND
NEIGHBOR
Beverly Crane
29 yrs., 3/79
SISTER-IN-LAW
Bill Martin
33 yrs.
11/77
SISTER, BROTHER-IN-LAW
Dick Frank
42 yrs., 2/77
Ron, Pam Dickson
25, 24 yrs
2/79

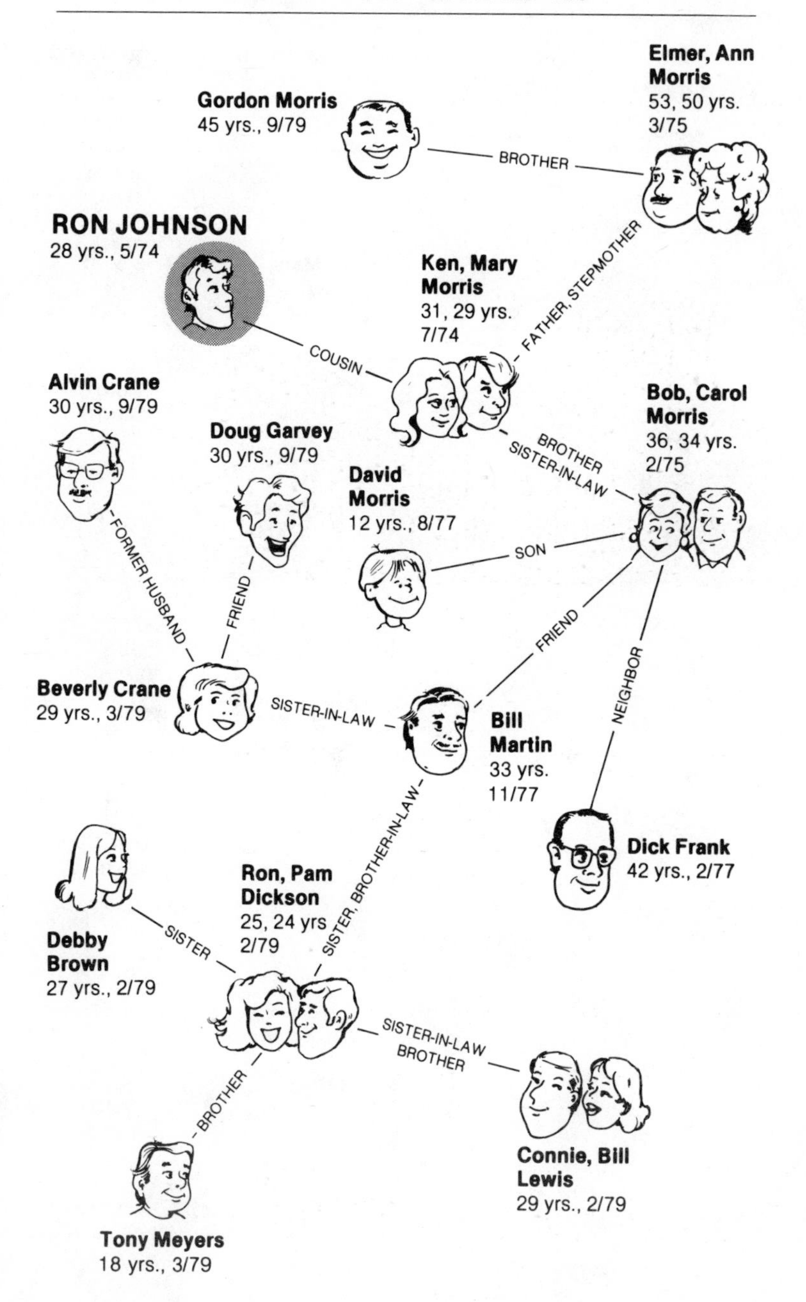
Elmer, Ann Morris
53, 50 yrs.
3/75
Gordon Morris
45 yrs., 9/79
BROTHER
RON JOHNSON
28 yrs., 5/74
Ken, Mary Morris
31, 29 yrs.
7/74
FATHER, STEPMOTHER
COUSIN
Alvin Crane
30 yrs., 9/79
Bob, Carol Morris
36, 34 yrs.
2/75
Doug Garvey
30 yrs., 9/79
BROTHER
SISTER-IN-LAW
David Morris
12 yrs., 8/77
SON
FORMER HUSBAND
FRIEND
FRIEND
NEIGHBOR
Beverly Crane
29 yrs., 3/79
SISTER-IN-LAW
Bill Martin
33 yrs.
11/77
SISTER, BROTHER-IN-LAW
Dick Frank
42 yrs., 2/77
Ron, Pam Dickson
25, 24 yrs
2/79
Debby Brown
27 yrs., 2/79
SISTER
SISTER-IN-LAW
BROTHER
BROTHER
Connie, Bill Lewis
29 yrs., 2/79
Tony Meyers
18 yrs., 3/79

Here is a second web that was traced in the church and continues to grow today.

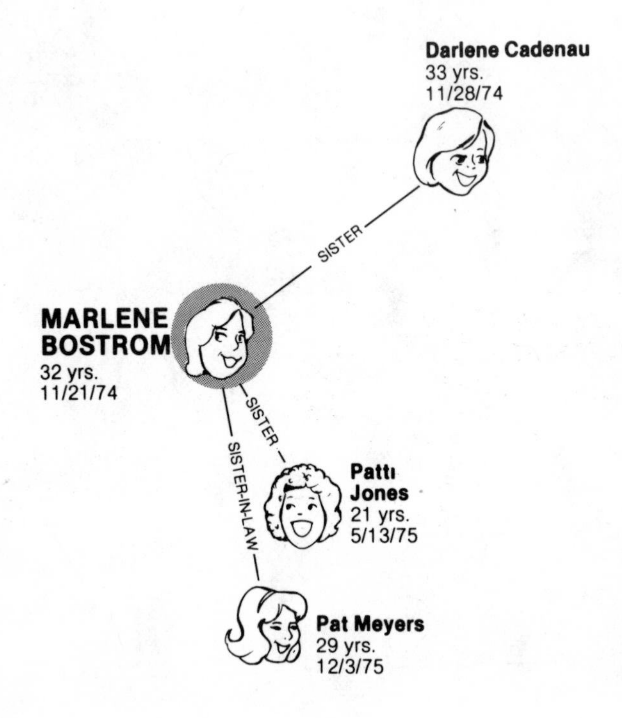

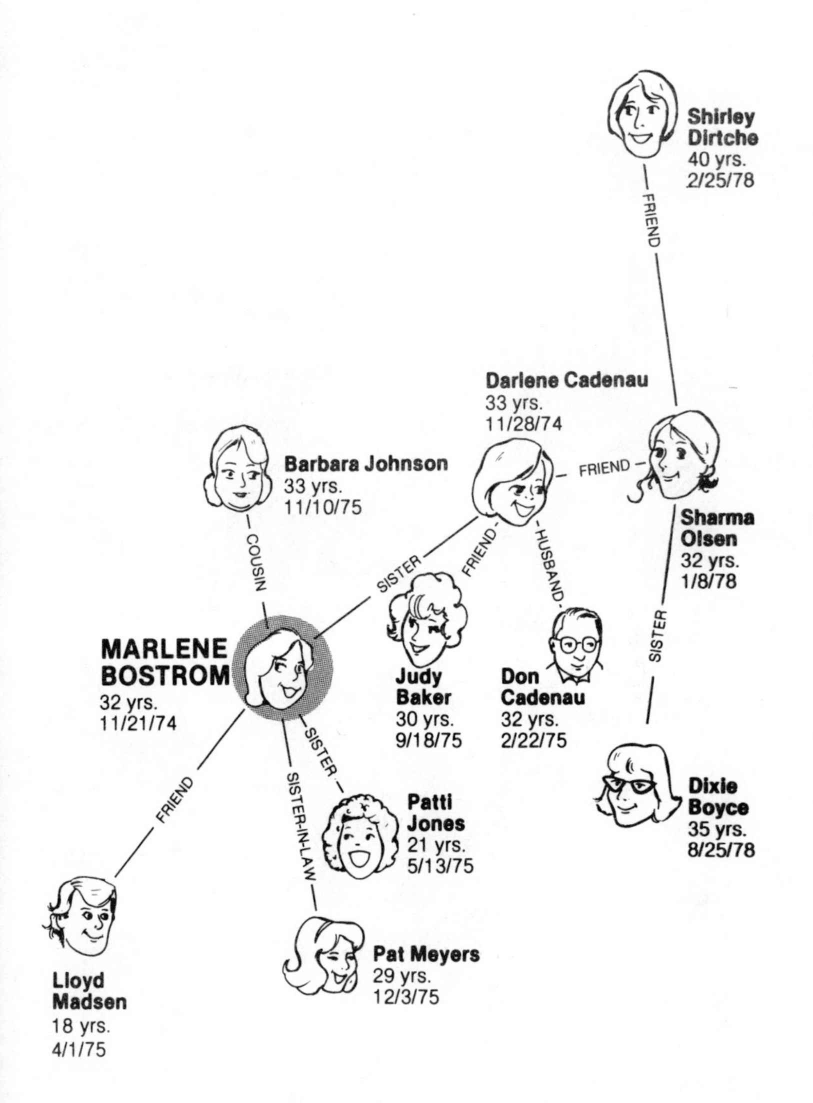
Shirley
Dirtche
40 yrs.
2/25/78
FRIEND
Darlene Cadenau
33 yrs.
11/28/74
FRIEND
Sharma
Olsen
32 yrs.
1/8/78
Barbara Johnson
33 yrs.
11/10/75
COUSIN
SISTER
FRIEND
HUSBAND
SISTER
MARLENE
BOSTROM
32 yrs.
11/21/74
Judy
Baker
30 yrs.
9/18/75
Don
Cadenau
32 yrs.
2/22/75
Dixie
Boyce
35 yrs.
8/25/78
FRIEND
SISTER
SISTER-IN-LAW
Patti
Jones
21 yrs.
5/13/75
Pat Meyers
29 yrs.
12/3/75
Lloyd
Madsen
18 yrs.
4/1/75

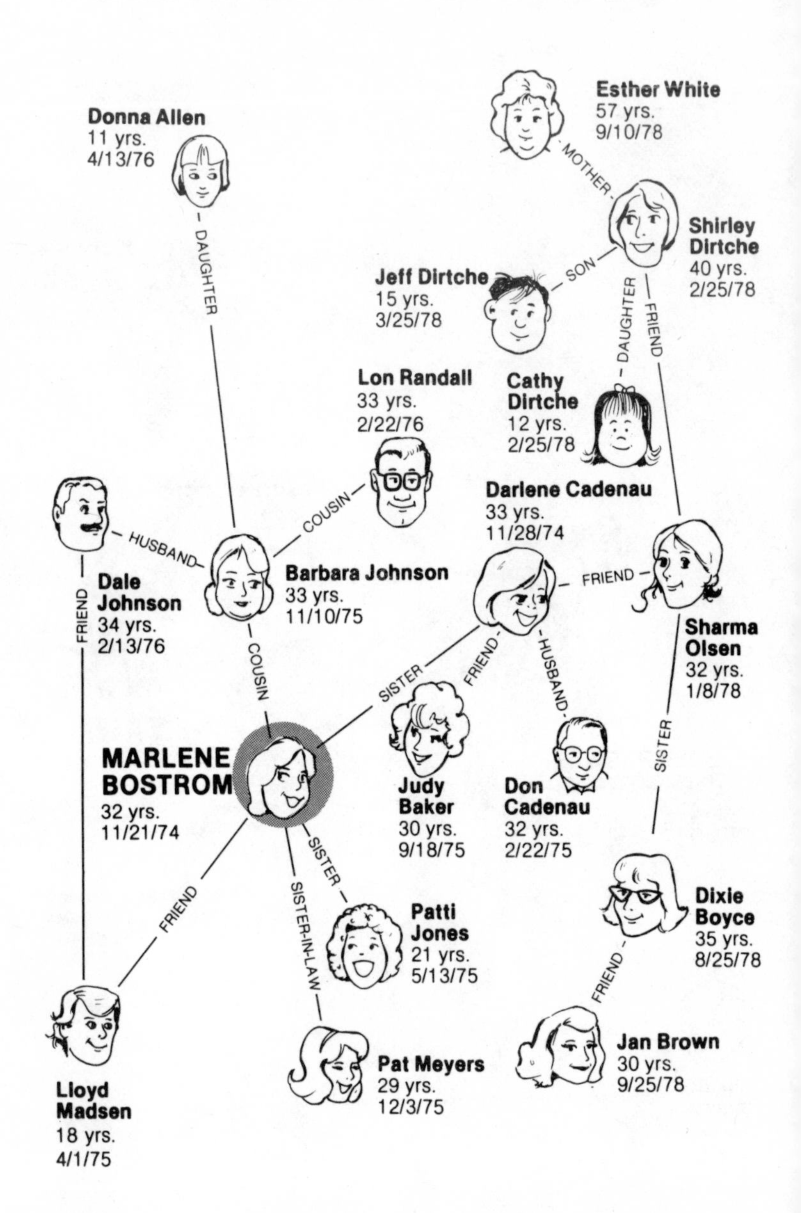
Esther White
57 yrs.
9/10/78
MOTHER
Donna Allen
11 yrs.
4/13/76
DAUGHTER
Shirley Dirtche
40 yrs.
2/25/78
SON
Jeff Dirtche
15 yrs.
3/25/78
DAUGHTER
FRIEND
Lon Randall
33 yrs.
2/22/76
Cathy Dirtche
12 yrs.
2/25/78
COUSIN
Darlene Cadenau
33 yrs.
11/28/74
HUSBAND
Dale Johnson
34 yrs.
2/13/76
Barbara Johnson
33 yrs.
11/10/75
FRIEND
FRIEND
Sharma Olsen
32 yrs.
1/8/78
COUSIN
SISTER
FRIEND
HUSBAND
SISTER
MARLENE BOSTROM
32 yrs.
11/21/74
Judy Baker
30 yrs.
9/18/75
Don Cadenau
32 yrs.
2/22/75
SISTER
SISTER-IN-LAW
FRIEND
Dixie Boyce
35 yrs.
8/25/78
Patti Jones
21 yrs.
5/13/75
FRIEND
Jan Brown
30 yrs.
9/25/78
Pat Meyers
29 yrs.
12/3/75
Lloyd Madsen
18 yrs.
4/1/75

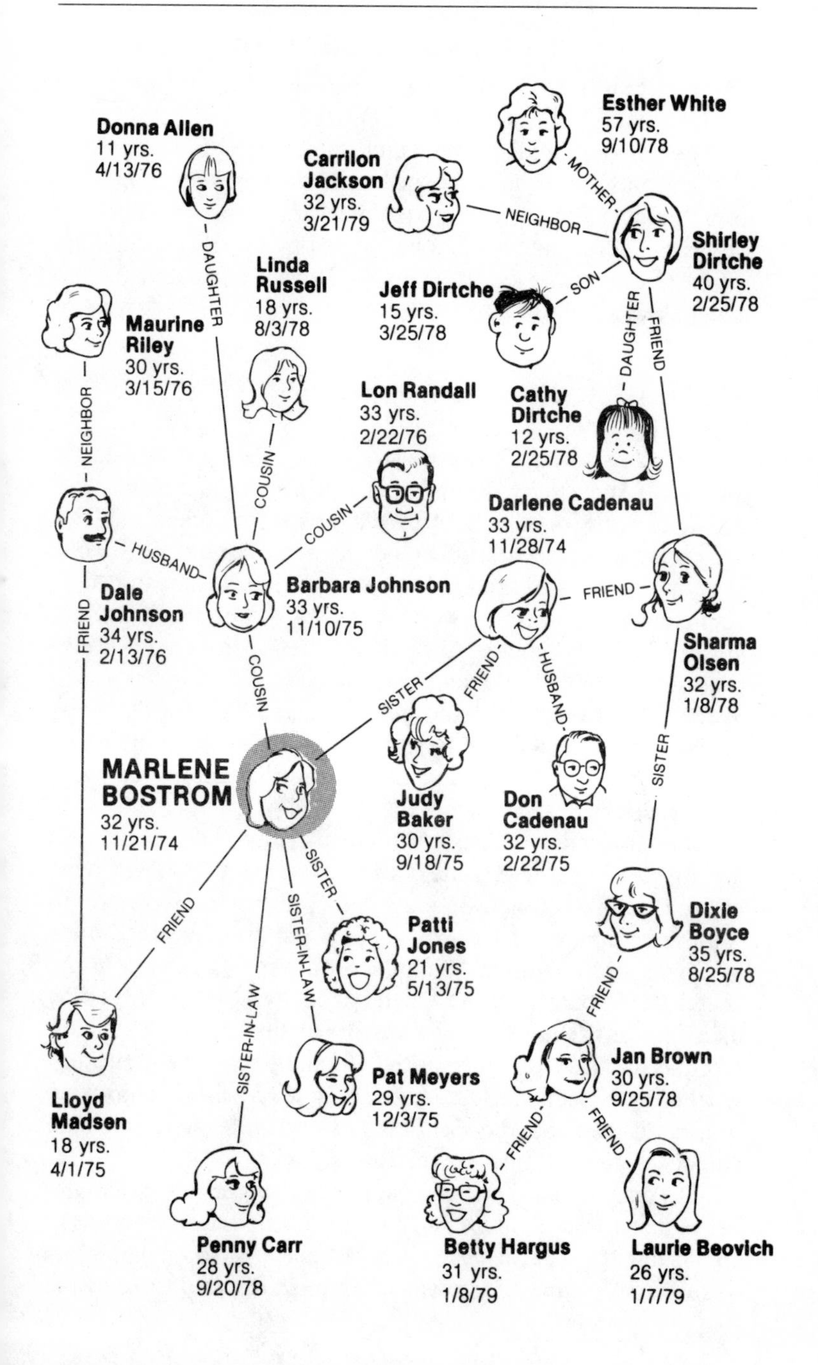
Esther White
57 yrs.
9/10/78
Donna Allen
11 yrs.
4/13/76
Carrilon Jackson
32 yrs.
3/21/79
MOTHER
NEIGHBOR
Shirley Dirtche
40 yrs.
2/25/78
Linda Russell
18 yrs.
8/3/78
Jeff Dirtche
15 yrs.
3/25/78
SON
DAUGHTER
DAUGHTER
FRIEND
Maurine Riley
30 yrs.
3/15/76
NEIGHBOR
Lon Randall
33 yrs.
2/22/76
Cathy Dirtche
12 yrs.
2/25/78
COUSIN
COUSIN
Darlene Cadenau
33 yrs.
11/28/74
HUSBAND
Dale Johnson
34 yrs.
2/13/76
Barbara Johnson
33 yrs.
11/10/75
FRIEND
FRIEND
Sharma Olsen
32 yrs.
1/8/78
COUSIN
SISTER
FRIEND
HUSBAND
SISTER
MARLENE BOSTROM
32 yrs.
11/21/74
Judy Baker
30 yrs.
9/18/75
Don Cadenau
32 yrs.
2/22/75
SISTER
FRIEND
SISTER-IN-LAW
Patti Jones
21 yrs.
5/13/75
Dixie Boyce
35 yrs.
8/25/78
SISTER-IN-LAW
FRIEND
Jan Brown
30 yrs.
9/25/78
Pat Meyers
29 yrs.
12/3/75
Lloyd Madsen
18 yrs.
4/1/75
FRIEND
FRIEND
Penny Carr
28 yrs.
9/20/78
Betty Hargus
31 yrs.
1/8/79
Laurie Beovich
26 yrs.
1/7/79

## STRATEGY FOR GROWTH

The fact that a great majority of people come to Christ and the local church through webs of relationships has great implications for your Sunday School and your church.

The following seven strategies are important keys to moving your Sunday School and church forward using the principle of webs. These strategies can be applied by any Sunday School seriously desiring to be obedient to Christ's command to "go and make disciples."

*STRATEGY 1—Design Sunday School Strategy around Webs of Growth.*

Webs are social ties between people. They are immediate family ties and extended family ties. They are relationships with people at work or at school or play. They are friendship ties and common interest ties. The people most responsive to your Sunday School outreach efforts and most likely to be added to your church will be found within the webs of members presently in your Sunday School. And when a new person comes into your Sunday School, it does more than add one additional person to the roll. It opens a brand new untapped web consisting of the person's friends and family now outside the church and Sunday School. The Sunday School desiring growth is enormously interested in all such webs.

The Gracemont Baptist Church of Tulsa, Oklahoma, has developed an excellent strategy that uses webs for growth. One of the first things a new Sunday School member is asked to do is list three families of his acquaintance that are presently outside of Christ and a church. Within several weeks a deacon in the church accompanies this new member on a visit to share his new discovery of life in Christ and why he or she became a member of Gracemont. According to Rev. Jimmy Reese, "The strategy is working tremendously," and the Sunday School is growing at a rapid pace. Sunday Schools grow when leaders, teachers, and departments emphasize reaching webs.

The diagram on the facing page shows two important insights about the growth of your church through the Sunday School. The first is that the cost (of time, energy, money, personnel) becomes increasingly greater as growth efforts are directed beyond the immediate webs and relationships of the member. The second insight is that results will be much greater when evangelistic strategy is directed toward immediate friends and extended families of members.

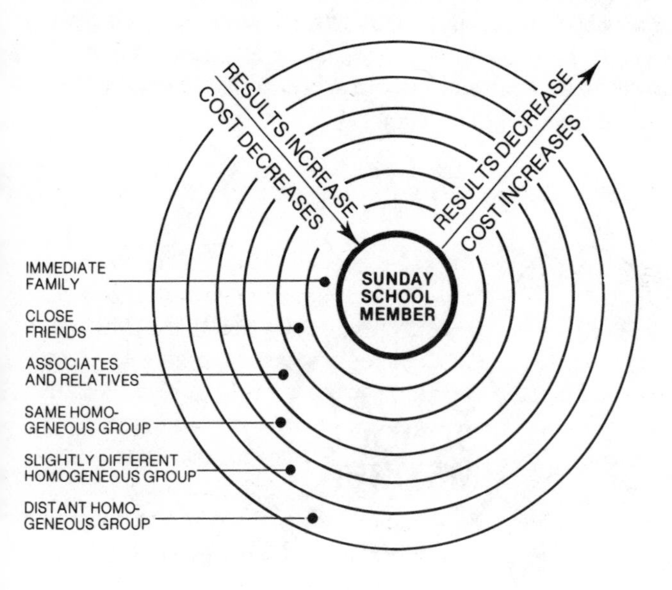


*STRATEGY 2—Identify Unreached People in the Webs of Present Members.*

In researching unreached people and webs of present church members, Robert Orr, minister of the Ness Avenue Baptist Church in Winnepeg, Manitoba, analyzed a variety of different churches. He discovered that, on the average, each member had 8.4 contacts—unchurched friends, relatives, work or school associates, interest groups and neighbors—in his or her web of influence. In older congregations, and with members who had been Christians for many years, that average dropped to approximately four contacts per member. In new congregations, and with newer Christians, the number grew to twelve.[19] Similar research was conducted by Rev. Wayne McDill with a sampling of Southern Baptist churches in Texas. His findings were almost identical.[20]

Enormous possibilities are presently available to most Sunday Schools if they build a prospect list composed of these people! A Sunday School of 200 members, for example, could easily compile a prospect list of 1000 to 2000 people! For an adult class of say 35, there could be a prospect list of nearly 300!

Below is an illustration of where prospects may be found:

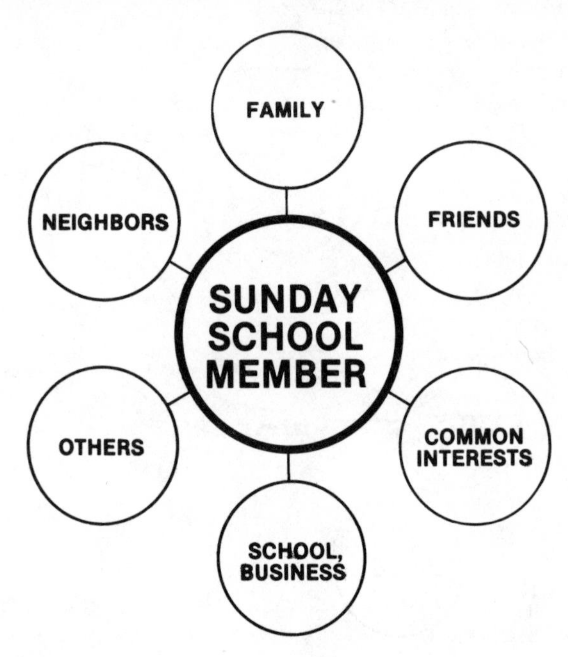


What do you then do with your prospect list?

The First United Methodist Church of Anderson, Indiana, has developed a "Caring System" that helps identify and respond to the particular needs of each person on their prospect list.[21] Individuals or families are identified, and a "Caring Committee" then develops a profile on the needs or problems that person or family may be facing, and the various ways the church might respond to and meet those needs. The church develops individual steps of strategy for contacting the family or individual, meeting their needs through the church, and inviting them to the Church

School and involvement in the life of the church. Each active member in the congregation is seen as a resource to help make this caring system work. Such a list of specific prospects and a strategy for each prospect is a proven way to growth in the church and Sunday School.

*STRATEGY 3—Disciple to the Fringes.*

Let's suppose you are the teacher of a class of 35 people. In your class is Mary Smith. If we assume that Mary is a typical class member, she has eight friends and associates in her web who are not presently in Christ or the church. A diagram of Mary's particular web would look like this:

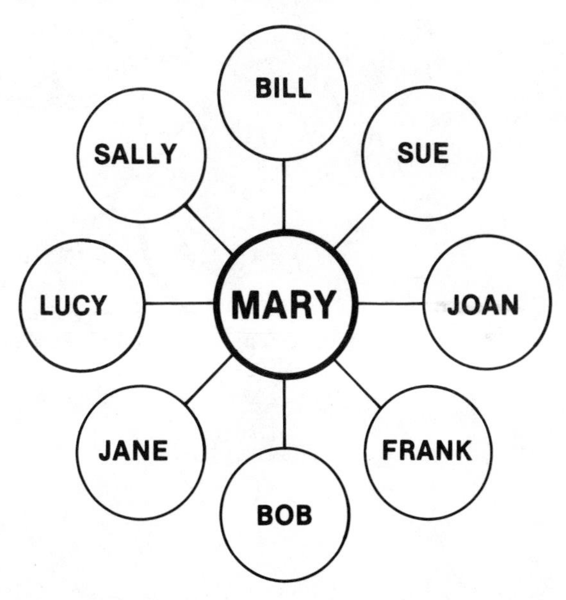


Let's assume that six months after Mary identified these people, she was instrumental in seeing three—Bill, Jane, and her husband Bob—make a Christian commitment and become members of the church and Sunday School. The principle of "discipling to the fringes" directs attention not only to Mary's web of eight people, but immediately enlarges to include the webs of Bill, Jane, and Bob. So, a second diagram of this expanding web now looks like this:

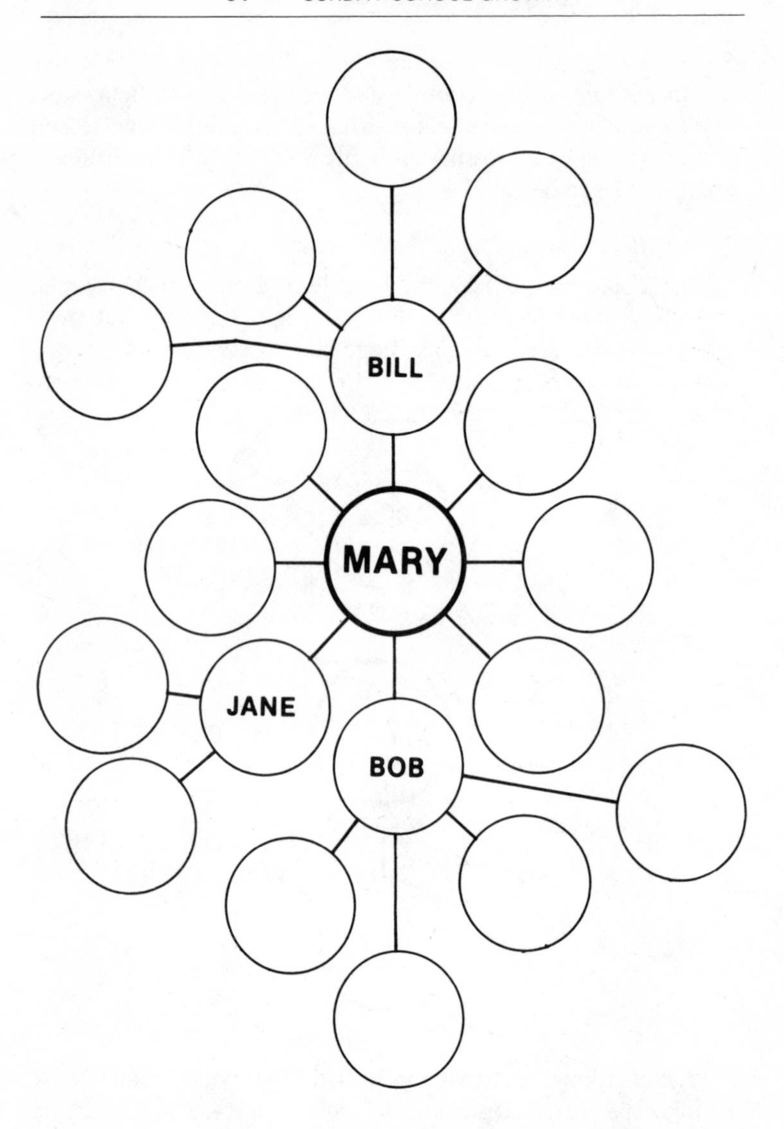


Bridges have been built from Mary to a growing number of other prospects, counting those in Bill's, Jane's and Bob's webs of influence. Yet, beyond that web are additional webs of readily accessible people, waiting to be added to your Sunday School prospect list.

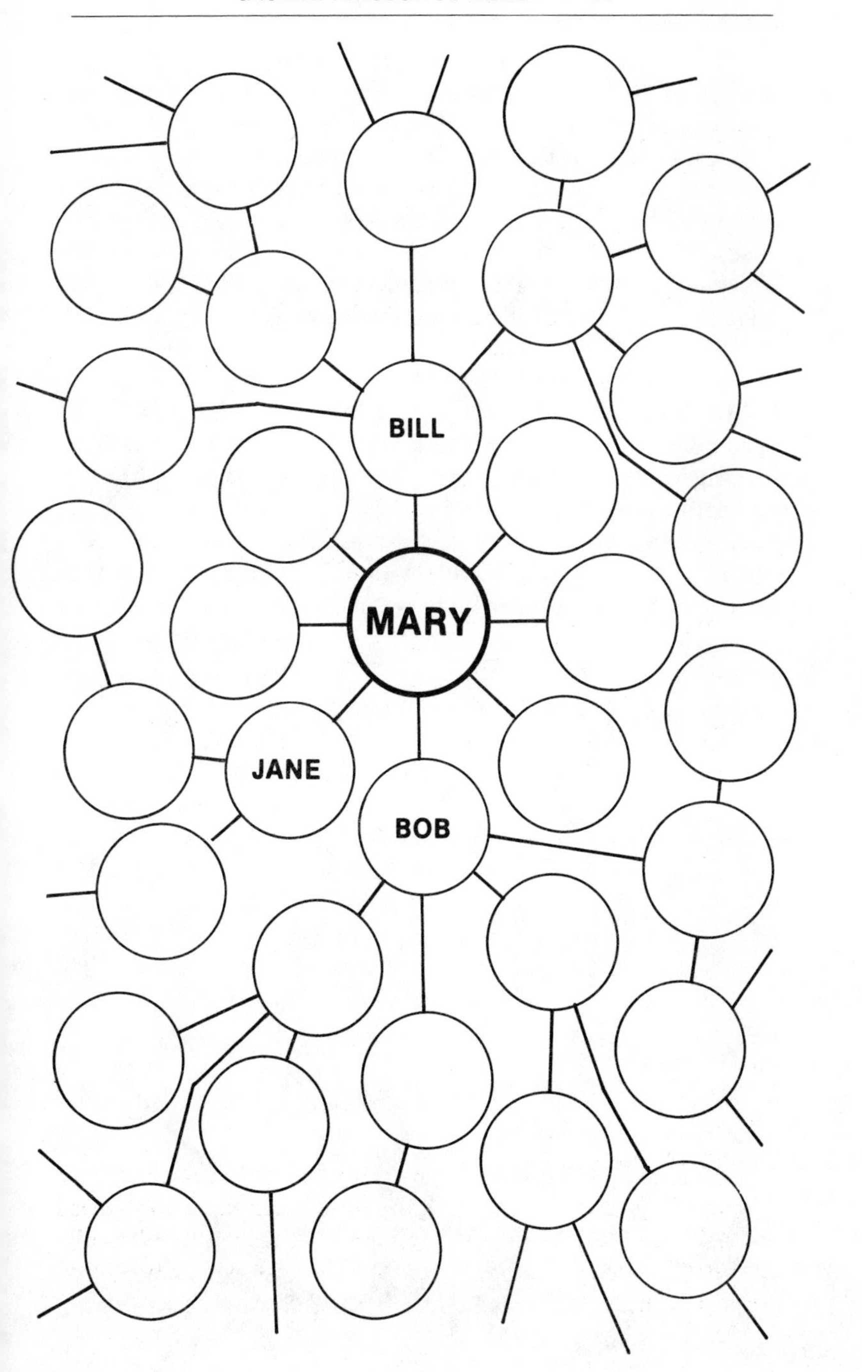
BILL
MARY
JANE
BOB

It was precisely this pattern that caused the New Testament church to explode. The *oikos* pattern continues to be the most natural and effective means of reaching people today. However, it is not enough just to know of these patterns. Specific strategies and plans and procedures must be established to follow these webs to the fringes, discipling men and women in the process. Of course, not all will be won, but there is no more receptive "soil" available than in these webs. When they are identified and worked, the harvest will be great.

*STRATEGY 4—Utilize New Converts.*

Closely related to Strategy 3 is the importance of new converts. The reason is that new converts open doors for growth often denied to established members. The diagram below illustrates a surprising yet natural phenomenon that occurs in every church and Sunday School. The circle represents the church. The pyramid represents the world. A person at the bottom of the pyramid represents a person in the world but outside of the church.

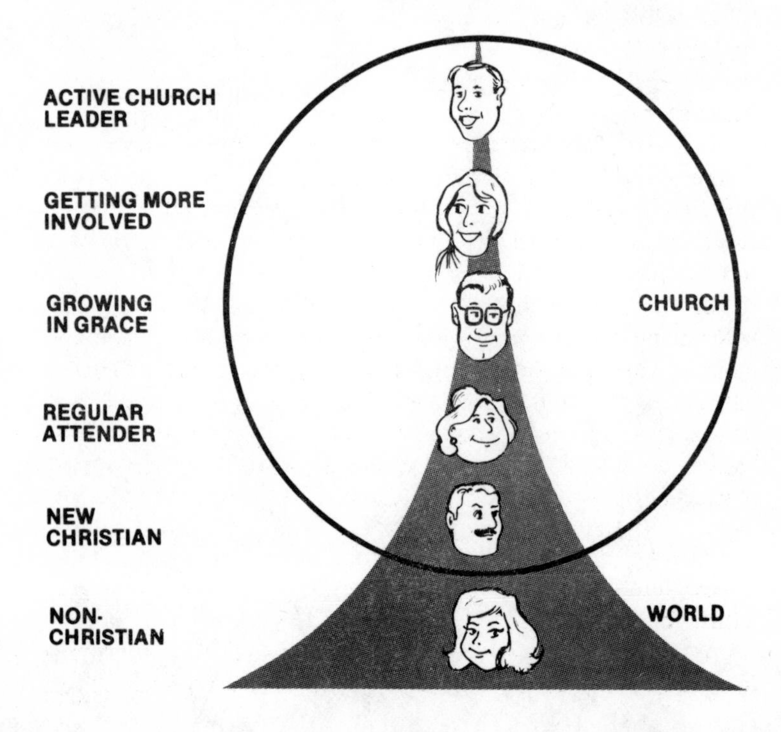

When the person becomes a Christian and a church member, he/she still has a good number of contacts and friends in the world. As time passes, however, the now older Christian maintains fewer and fewer contacts in the world, and more and more contacts in the church. The reason is simply that as a Christian, he feels more comfortable associating with other Christians. His new life in Christ is not compatible with the lifesytyle of his old friends outside the church.

Many growing Sunday Schools have discovered this fact that new converts have a great many more contacts with unchurched prospects than do long-time members, and have found ways to effectively train them to share this new life with their friends.

An often told story in church growth circles is of Mary, a twenty-eight year old, flaming red-haired, divorcee cocktail waitress. When Mary became a Christian, the first thing she did was walk over to the phone, dial her boss and say, "I quit." She saw no way to be a Christian and a cocktail waitress. Prior to her baptism, Mary sent out engraved invitations to all the "old crowd" to come and see her be baptized. That night the first seven rows of the church were full. (You know those people had never been to church before or they wouldn't have sat there!)

Following her baptism there was a reception in a home, where Mary, her former friends, her new church friends, and the pastor all gathered. During the evening, Mary gave her testimony and her pastor told what it meant to be in Christ and in the church.

In the next six months following her baptism, Mary was instrumental in bringing ten of her friends to Christ and the church. The second six months she helped lead five others to Christ and the church. However, the second year she didn't lead anyone to Christ and the church. Why? She was out of contacts! All her friends were in the church. While Mary's new Christian friends still had many contacts, Mary did not.

*STRATEGY 5—Win Family Units.*

An important part of using webs for growth is to win entire families. Why?

A) A natural bridge exists to those outside of Christ and the church through the family member(s) already participating.

B) Family members are often winnable and very responsive when properly approached.

C) If the family is not won, the possibilities of the one Christian family member eventually dropping out of the church increase tremendously. (Thousands of churches that emphasize a bus ministry to children will readily testify to the great losses that occur unless the entire family is won.)

D) When the whole family is in Christ and the church, its supportive system in the home provides encouragement, unity, and Christian growth. The opposite is often true in the non-Christian home.

E) The family itself is strengthened when all members are moving in the same direction, rather than creating division and fragmentation.

Applying this step is easy. Identify children, youth, and adults who presently attend alone. Then analyze each one in relationship to his or her family needs, backgrounds, receptivity, and location. Develop individual plans which hold promise of reaching this family, based on the various factors in each situation.

The Grace Baptist Church of Mahomet, Illinois, has developed a way of building a bridge from the children involved in activities of the church to parents who are not attending. Lay members are enlisted to make a friendly visit to the home and introduce themselves to the parents. They explain that the church is evaluating the effectiveness of its programs and would like the parents to fill out a questionnaire on what they feel to be the benefits of their daughter or son's involvement. Do they have any recommendations for making the program more beneficial to the children? The parents are not asked about their own beliefs or worship patterns. They are simply asked to complete the questionnaire and mail it back to the church. The pastor will often drop a note of thanks to the parents for responding and encourage them to communicate with him any time they would like. The goal of the program is to establish contact with parents, add them to the prospect list, and begin to build bridges to the entire family.

*STRATEGY 6—Build New Webs.*

You will remember from Strategy 4, that when left to natural patterns, the long-time Christian maintains fewer and fewer contacts with non-Christians. Does this mean older Christians are absolved of responsibility to reach new people? Of course not. But it does mean that a deliberate strategy must be built to create *new* webs.

Many growing Sunday Schools have developed creative ways to build new webs from present members to new people outside the church. Here is an example of how this principle is working:

The United Methodist Church in Carmel, Indiana, has developed a successful strategy of identifying and reaching out to people who first move into its ministry area. The community is divided into areas, sections, and sub-sections on a large map in the church, and on smaller copies of the map for each member. One person or family from the church is assigned to a particular sub-section. (Members are always assigned to a sub-section in which they live.) These sub-sections are several blocks long. The members are then responsible for staying alert to any new people or families that move into their subsection. Members are encouraged to immediately introduce themselves, welcome the new neighbors, invite them to dinner, develop a friendship, and be alert to ways the church can respond and reach out to these new people. The program, according to Rev. Dale Miller, is a major factor in the consistent growth of the church and church school.

*STRATEGY 7—Pray for Unreached Webs.*

There is power in prayer. Constant, earnest prayer is vital for Sunday School growth. Not simply vague utterances for a more Christian world or a return to our Christian heritage. But a sincere, fervent petitioning of God for specific individuals outside Christ and the church. Prayer for people—by name—who are in our webs of influence. Prayer that these people might be reached and discipled into the Body of Christ.

Scripture abounds with promises that if we but ask in His name, He will hear and answer. Sunday Schools and churches *grow* when prayer is specific, for people and for growth.[22]

The Grace Baptist Church of Newhall, California, discovered this important principle. Following weeks of preparation, planning and prayer, members of the church were asked to list, on a card, non-Christian friends and relatives for whom they would pray during the next year. On one communion Sunday morning, members put these cards on the altar at the front of the church, a symbol of the covenant they had made with God, to pray for those people. The staff distributed the names to individual prayer groups throughout the church, so that they were then regularly prayed for by church members. From the initial prospect list of over 800 names, 276 have found Christ as Lord and Savior, and every month the church is baptizing new people and welcoming them into the fellowship.

Understanding the principle of webs is an important concept for the teachers, leaders, and members in your Sunday School. Identifying and evangelizing along these webs is a proven and effective way to "find the lost" and turn potential new members into comrades of the cross.

## FOOTNOTES

### CHAPTER FIVE

1. Acts 16:12
2. Donald McGavran, *The Bridges of God* (New York: Friendship Press, 1955, p. 26.
3. Romans 1:16
4. Acts 16:12-15
5. Acts 16:23-31
6. Thomas A. Wolf, "The Biblical Pattern of Effective Evangelism," in *The Pastor's Church Growth Handbook,* ed. Win Arn (Pasadena: Church Growth Press, 1979), p. 112.
7. Charles Lowry, "Oikos Evangelism" (research project, New Orleans Baptist Seminary, December 1979).
8. Michael Green, *Evangelism in the Early Church* (Grand Rapids: Eerdmans, 1970), p. 210.
9. For a detailed study of the homogeneous unit principle and church growth, see Peter Wagner, *Our Kind Of People* (Atlanta: John Knox, 1979).
10. Wolf, op. cit., p. 115.
11. A similar study was conducted by Charles Lowry as part of a research project with the New Orleans Baptist Seminary. ("Oikos Evangelism," December, 1979.) After surveying 400 pastors, his findings to the question, "Who was responsible for the initial contact [which resulted in your now being a member of the church]?" were: Family member = 67%, Friends/neighbors = 13%, Sunday School or Vacation Bible School = 11%, Pastor/staff = 7%. Note the total of 80% friends/relatives.
12. Warren Hartman, *Membership Trends: A Study of Decline and Growth in the United Methodist Church, 1949-1975* Nashville: Discipleship Re-

sources, 1976, p. 6), found that 62% of the professions of faith in the United Methodist Church came through the Church School. Charles Lowry (op. cit., p. 15) found that among the Southern Baptists he surveyed, 58% said the Sunday School was the part of the church they first came into contact with.

13. DECISION, Billy Graham Evangelistic Association (August, 1976).
14. Win Arn, "Mass Evangelism: The Bottom Line" CHURCH GROWTH: AMERICA 4, no. 1 (January/February 1978).
15. Bill Bright, in a speech at the Anaheim Convention Center, delivered December 11, 1976 (Anaheim, California), said "I believe that one can truthfully say that here in the United States the Great Commission will be fulfilled by the end of this year."
16. Win Arn, "A Church Growth Look at Here's Life, America!" CHURCH GROWTH: AMERICA 3, no. 1 (January/February 1977).
17. C. Peter Wagner, "Who Found It?" ETERNITY 28, no. 9 (September, 1979).
18. The names in these examples have been changed, but do, in fact, represent actual people now in this church.
19. Robert Orr, "How to Develop a Prospect List . . ." CHURCH GROWTH: AMERICA 5, no. 4 (September/October 1979).
20. Wayne McDill, *Making Friends For Christ* (Nashville: Broadman, 1979), p. 29.
21. Donald La Suer, and Ray Sells, *The Caring System* (Pasadena: Christian Communication, 1979).
22. At this writing a unique new application of the principle of webs was being developed by Christian Communication, entitled, "The Sharing and Caring Network." The kit will be a practical way for a local Sunday School and/or church to introduce the principle of webs to members, and develop a practical strategy for implementing the principle for growth. Information on the Sharing and Caring Network may be obtained by writing Christian Communication, 150 S. Los Robles, #600, Pasadena, California 91101.

CHAPTER SIX

# GROWTH: THROUGH ASSIMILATION

Bill and Mary McKay had high expectations as they walked down the aisle to become new members of the church. A few weeks earlier, the pastor had led Bill and Mary to Christ. Now, after testifying to their new faith, they turned to face the congregation, and the pastor, on behalf of the church, welcomed them into the membership. The people were smiling and obviously pleased to have Bill and Mary join their church. Many of the members nodded to them as they returned to their seats. They were both very happy and looking forward to a long, growing relationship with the people in their new church.

Eleven months later, after those warm words of welcome and reception into membership, Bill and Mary McKay were inactive. They had not been to worship in two months and would probably not attend the church again. There was no falling out with the pastor or people. There was no conflict in theology. The problem was that Bill and Mary had never been incorporated into the life and fellowship of that church. What was worse, few people even knew they had drifted out the back door. When they joined the church, Bill and Mary had no intention of dropping out. But they did.

What happened?

Why did this seemingly happy marriage between new members and the congregation sour into separation and divorce? What happens in a great many other churches that see Bills and Marys disappear from active membership roles? Can the trend be changed? Can the Sunday School have a role in reducing the drop-out problem many churches face, and help new members become assimilated into the life and fellowship of the Body?

The answer is a resounding "Yes!"

This chapter sets forth important principles of church growth which, when applied, will greatly aid in incorporating new people and show how your Sunday School can make a most important contribution to the process of successful assimilation.

## THE SUNDAY SCHOOL— EFFECTIVE RESOURCE FOR INCORPORATION

Let's first look at *why* the Sunday School is so uniquely qualified to incorporate new members. Here are eight reasons . . .

1) *The Sunday School builds bridges of friendship and relationships.* Friendship is the most important key in binding new members to each other and to the church. The stronger and more meaningful these relationships become, the more assured you can be that these people will become and continue to be active Christians in Sunday School and church.

The "belonging factor" is of major importance in understanding the process of assimilation.[1] Sunday School leaders and teachers often assume that the primary function of their Sunday School is to teach the Bible. They believe the Sunday School's greatest contribution to the Body is biblical literacy and application of biblical truth. While this is certainly a major contribution of the Sunday School, the primary factors which affect people's continued participation and involvement in their Sunday School are *relationships with others, their sense of belonging, and social fellowship.*[2]

Lake Avenue Congregational Church, (Pasadena, CA), an excellent example of a church using its Sunday School classes to weld new people to the life of the church, spells out one of the major functions of the education classes in their philosophy of ministry statement: "They are to function relationally, as congregations, providing the necessary feeling of belonging and togetherness, providing social functions appropriate for each age level, providing social concern and practical care for the members."[3]

Several intriguing research studies support the fact that people's participation in Sunday School depends on the existence of or the lack of relationships .

One such study found that the number of close friends a person develops in the Sunday School has a direct relationship to that person's own involvement in the Sunday School. If a person has few or no close friends in the Sunday School, the chances are quite low that he will be active in the Sunday School. If an individual has many close friends in the Sunday School, that person will have an active level of involvement.[4]

The importance of friendship in the Sunday School can be seen in another study. It compared 50 new members who were still active six months after joining, with 50 new members who dropped out after six months. The new members who stayed and were incorporated had made more than seven new friends in the church and Sunday School. Those who dropped out had made less than two.[5]

Additional evidence which shows the important relationship between friendship and successful assimilation comes from interviews with Sunday School drop-outs.

These people were asked: 1) Why they dropped out of Sunday School, and 2) What would most influence their choice of a new church home? The answer regularly given to question #1 was "Did not feel part of the group." The response to the second question, given by a majority of the people, was "Friendliness of the people."[6]

The Sunday School is ideally suited for building new friendships and a sense of belonging. Sunday Schools successful in assimilating new members have found ways to actively encourage the development of close friendships among the members as a means of cementing a long-term relationship to the church.

2) *The Sunday School expands the opportunities for task and role involvement.* Suppose you are part of a church of 300 members. If yours is typical, approximately 80 opportunities now exist for members to become involved in a role or task; that

is, to serve on a committee, teach a class, or get involved in some other way. Sixty of these roles will be filled by 10% of the laity. The remaining 20 roles are filled by another 20 people. The result . . . five-sixths of the church members have *no role* in your church. Those who eventually leave out the "back door" of your church will come almost entirely from this group.

The difference between the number of members in your church and the number of available roles to be filled by laity is important to understand. There is a direct relationship between the number of new people a church can incorporate and the number of roles that exist in that church. A church with a high number of roles or tasks to be filled by lay people assimilates a much greater percentage of new members than the church with large numbers of members and few opportunities for participation.

This principle is true for any church—small, medium or large. It is quite possible, for example, to have a congregation of 150 members or less and a very low involvement level of most members. This indicates that either not enough roles have been created, or that all the roles are taken by a small percentage of people. On the other hand, a church of 2,000 may have an excellent incorporation and involvement level because it has been able to add roles and tasks as membership grew. Some churches, in fact, have a strategy for growth that first creates new roles and then looks for new people to fill them!

In research conducted among 48 congregations, laity were asked to list the number of available roles, jobs, or task assignments they knew of in their congregation.[7] This number was compared to the total number of members in each church to determine the proportion of perceived roles to members. In rapidly growing congregations, the ratio was about 55:100; that is, they were aware of 55 jobs for each 100 members. In medium-growth-rate churches, 43 roles were listed for each 100 members. In low-growth-rate churches the perceived role-to-member ratio was 27 for each 100 members.

What kind of roles might the Sunday School be able to provide? The possibilities are vast. In an individual class there are opportunities to serve on committees (planning, social, curriculum, evangelism, special projects, incorporation, sports). There are regular duties (making announcements, taking attendance, being class representative, acting as a greeter, song leader, or missions coordinator). There are also opportunities to serve on general Sunday School committees (long-range planning, research, special events, new class development).

The Sunday School is uniquely able to create new roles. When a person is involved in a personally meaningful task, in most cases, he or she is quite likely to become a responsible church member.

3) *The Sunday School can provide a place for each person.* No other organization in the church has the ability to match nearly every prospect with a "like" group of people. In many Sunday Schools, singles can find a place, or divorced, or widowed, or high schoolers, or handicapped, or young couples . . . a Sunday School can have a place for all. Of course, not every Sunday School provides a place for all, but every Sunday School, if it so desired, *could* provide a place.

The "likeness" of a group to the new member or potential new member has a significant influence on whether that person will be successfully incorporated.[8] If the person has many points of common identity with the group, that person is much more likely to become an active member. When a person "drops out" of the church, it is often because there was no group where that person "fit."

A diagram helps to illustrate this truth (see following page). Mr. X comes through the front door as a new member. He is given the right hand of fellowship. He is told he is loved. He is given his offering envelopes. He is "in." Once in, Mr. X begins to look for a group to identify with.

I was once an X. I had received the right hand of fellowship along with my offering envelopes. I had been told how much I was loved and how happy I would be in the church. However, I soon discovered that groups of people who knew each other spent most of their time within those groups. They all "belonged." I didn't! Perhaps the problem was with me. I tried a few groups, and they were "friendly" but did not incorporate me. Eventually, I did what every other X does. I drifted out the back door. We don't speak much of the back door, but evangelism is ineffective if the front door and the back door are both wide open.

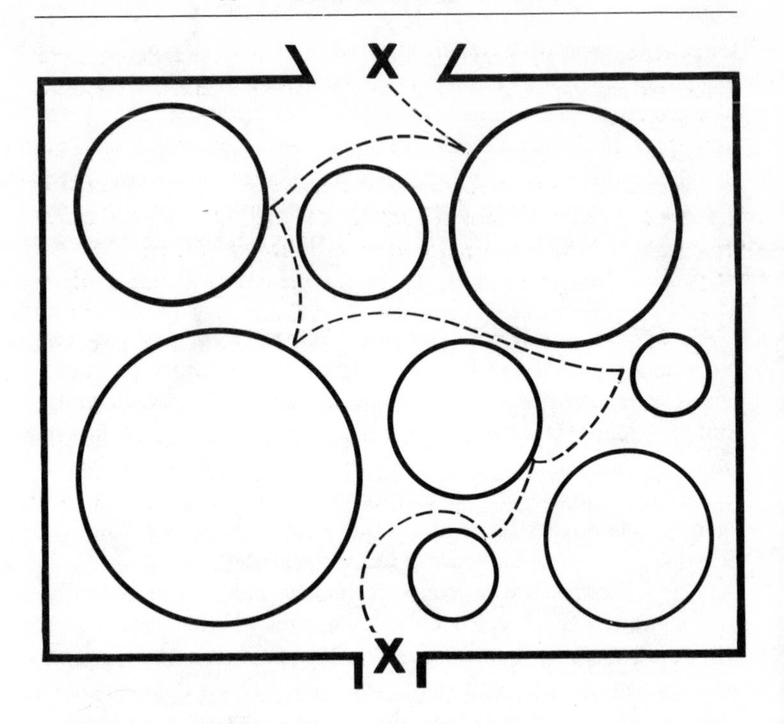


The Sunday School and the various classes are uniquely qualified to provide a place for each person, where they "fit."

4) *The Sunday School is organizationally suited for monitoring member involvement and providing responsive measures.* The new member's regularity of Sunday School attendance, his level of commitment, his development of new friendships, should all be closely monitored as he participates in the Sunday School system. These are the barometers for predicting a person's future participation level in the church. Research has shown that attendance in Sunday School is often the first indicator of a later pattern of worship attendance and church membership.[9] If a new member becomes a regular and active Sunday School attender, then regular worship attendance and church membership usually follow directly. But when a member begins to falter in his or her Sunday School attendance, it often is the first of several steps out the back door. Sunday Schools that closely monitor individual participation can take remedial

action which will prevent loss and promote warm, cordial relationships which lead "visitors" to become functioning parts of the Body.

Growing numbers of churches are developing a current file of information on each new member. The files are regularly reviewed, Sunday School attendance checked, stewardship trends observed, consultation made with teacher and others as to the progress of the individual in the incorporation process. If remedial action appears necessary, the Sunday School is in an ideal position to respond to the problem before it becomes irreversible.[10]

Dr. John Savage, in a doctoral study,[11] discovered that people often send out signals of dissatisfaction as an early step in the dropout process. A decrease in Sunday School attendance is one of the most frequent signals of people who are not happy. A Sunday School that closely watches for these signals can quickly respond to the problem and perhaps save much heartache later for both church and member.

5) *The Sunday School, through its class structure, provides accountability.* Behavior change is directly related to accountability. You are familiar with organizations which seek to change habit patterns of over-eaters, chronic alcohol drinkers, drug abusers, smokers, etc. All build strongly on accountability. When individuals make commitments to others for changing their own behavior, they are responsible both to themselves and to each other. Similarly, when a new convert or member is accountable to others through groups such as a Sunday School class, there is an important additional level of commitment to that goal.

6) *The Sunday School can provide a base for koinonia.* More than just organizational management or behavior principles are involved in seeing a person come into a new relationship with the Body of Christ. The Sunday School can provide strength that comes from mutual love, support, and encouragement of fellow believers. The spiritual camaraderie of fellow Christians wrestling with mutual problems and seeking to learn and grow together makes the Sunday School a highly effective instrument for incorporating new people.

*7) The Sunday School provides a bridge to worship.* For most Christians, Sunday morning is the focal point in the church calendar. It is that designated time when the people of God come together in worship. It is a time of church-wide celebration. It is the regular opportunity for the entire Body to rejoice in God. The worship service is the heartbeat of the local church. Since the Sunday School normally meets immediately before or after the worship service, it provides a natural bridge to participation in the important, mutually supportive, growing worship experience.

## PRINCIPLES FOR EFFECTIVE SUNDAY SCHOOL INCORPORATION

The Sunday School has many strengths that qualify it as an important incorporation agency of the local church. Here are five principles of incorporation and how your Sunday School can effectively apply them.

1. *An effective Sunday School builds an "incorporation consciousness."* A strong emphasis on incorporation within the Sunday School is the first step toward an effective incorporation strategy. As members, teachers and leaders of the Sunday School begin thinking about how to close the "back door," and become concerned with whether new members are finding a "home," the Sunday School's effectiveness is measured with a much more accurate yardstick.

The goal of incorporating new people must be given high priority and high visibility. The active involvement of new members must be a major agenda item for every Sunday School planning committee, officers' meeting, class and department session. Success should be measured not only by how many come in, but by how many become functioning, active parts of the group, and thus stay in.

Look for a moment at a different scenario for Bill and Mary McKay, the young couple who joined their church with such high hopes, but dropped out within the first year.

Suppose on that first Sunday the pastor had personally introduced them to two other young couples their age who invited Bill and Mary to attend Sunday School with them. In the class Bill and Mary were asked to introduce themselves and tell a little about their interests and background. Then, after church, suppose they had been asked over for dinner by a couple in the class. And later in the week, they had been invited to a basketball game with three other couples from the class. These gestures would probably have become the beginning of long-term friendships with others in the class. The story of Bill and Mary, eleven months later, would probably have been much different.

Here are some suggestions for raising the "incorporation consciousness" of your Sunday School:

• Establish a new member tracking committee of lay people exclusively concerned with overseeing the first nine months of the new member's life in the Sunday School. The committee keeps accurate records and updated information on every new Sunday School member or potential member. It provides information to each class or teacher when patterns of inactivity are discerned.

• Appoint a committee in each class that is responsible for the incorporation of new people. Such a committee accomplishes two important goals. It places responsiblity for incorporating new members on class members, and it provides additional roles of ministry to be filled. The committee is responsible to see that new members are meaningfully involved, and that the class is open to accept them.

• Create new roles and communicate them. Look for ways to match people—their interests, gifts, skills—with involvement in the church. If no such opportunities exist, create them. Communicate these opportunities to new people and encourage them in their new role.

• Research previous incorporation results. Graphing these results gives unique insights into the success or failure of classes in incorporating new people. Analyze the number of prospects who did and did not become active Sunday School members. Also investigate the one-year-old members and their present degree of participation in the Sunday School.

• Some Sunday Schools, in an effort to improve their incorporation of new members, interview once-active but now inactive members, to find out why they dropped out.[12] Lessons learned from these people are valuable in alleviating potential problems for new members.

2. *An effective Sunday School encourages homogeneous classes within the heterogeneous Body.* This principle is not new to the Sunday School. Many classes are formed according to age—a homogeneous characteristic. But in Sunday Schools with a high incorporation rate, the principle is applied beyond this superficial level. The important insight for effective incorporation is that *people enjoy being with other people like themselves.*[13] In most Sunday Schools, however, members' unique characteristics are ignored. The principle of homogeneity somehow seems to slip through the organizational cracks. When this happens, the Sunday School is inadvertantly saying, "You are all the same." The problem is that people in your Sunday School are not all the same. As adults mature, they develop special interests, goals, spiritual needs, and friendships which are quite different from those of other adults. To ignore these unique characteristics is to overlook one of the most important keys to effective assimilation.

An interesting study investigated this question of commonality and incorporation, and concluded that:

> Any effort to persuade a person to affiliate with a group is much more likely to be successful if the individual and the group already have some areas of potential identification.[14]

The study then examined the three factors of socio-economic status, age, and education level as they related to a church and Sunday School's ability to reach and incorporate people from the surrounding community. Concerning *socio-economic status,* churches and communities were placed in upper, upper-middle, middle, lower-middle, and lower socio-economic levels. It was found that high growth churches and Sunday Schools averaged one half of a socio-economic level above that of the people in their area. Medium growth churches were usually one-half level below their community. Low growth churches were more than two levels removed from most of the people in their community.[15] The socio-economic level of the church or the community had no bearing on church growth. However, the socio-economic relationships *between* the church and community, did have a significant influence on the ability of a church to reach and incorporate people.

Concerning *age,* it was found that the age of a person, by itself, had nothing to do with whether a person was a good prospect for membership. But the nearer a prospect's age was to the average age of the people in the group, the greater the chance of that person becoming an active and involved member. In high growth churches, the average age in the congregation was only two years and nine months above the average age in the community. In slow-growing churches, the average age was eleven years and nine months above the average age in the community.[16]

In analyzing *educational level,* five groups were identified, from high school dropouts to graduate degree holders. In rapidly-growing churches the average education level was only about one half a level above that of the community. In churches with a low growth rate, there was a difference of more than two educational levels between the church and the community.[17]

There are other common denominators that directly influence the ability of a Sunday School to incorporate new people: special interests, occupation, common problems, place of residence, ethnic background, language, common goals, family and marital status. Not all items will affect assimilation equally. Some will have more influence in a particular Sunday School class than others. However, as you seek to integrate prospects and new members into the life of the Sunday School—and therefore of the church—the "match" between the person and the group should be carefully considered. When it is impossible to find a "match," you have an excellent reason to start a new group. (More about this later.) The basic principle is this: the more *heterogeneous* the Sunday School is, as a whole, the wider its potential appeal. The more *homogeneous* the classes are, the better the chances of successful incorporation of people.

When a Sunday School department provides a wide range of groups, electives, and roles, its potential for incorporating many kinds of people is greatly increased.

3. *An effective Sunday School knows the saturation point of each class.* Evidence substantiates the fact that Sunday School classes have a "saturation point" beyond which they cannot grow.[18]

The Southern Baptists, on the basis of considerable study of the Sunday School, suggest class enrollment ceilings for every young people's group and adult class. When these attendance figures are reached, a new class is immediately started.[19]

Dr. Peter Wagner, church growth professional, studied the classes in the Lake Avenue Congregational Church and found an interesting phenomenon. In plotting the growth of adult Sunday School classes in this church of 3,000 members, he observed a pattern of growth—up to a certain numerical point. When the growth line passed beyond a certain level, and approached this "saturation point," attendance became erratic and soon dropped below that level. When growth later began again, it continued until it approached this apparent saturation point. Then it dropped again. In this particular instance, the level for these large adult classes was approximately 150.[20]

The figure will be different for each church and Sunday School class. It will be smaller for younger children than for older children or adults. But discovering the maximum growth potential of each class is important. Here's how: observe the recent growth patterns of each of your Sunday School classes. If you can see a number beyond which growth seems to hesitate or stop, you have begun to identify the "saturation level" for that class. Lake Avenue Church found that when attendance in their classes began approaching the saturation level it was a clear signal to organize a new class.

4. *An effective Sunday School makes a conscious effort to be open to newcomers.* Sociologists know that long-established groups can easily become closed to outsiders. The longer any group has been in existence, the more difficult it is for an outsider to break in . . . the more traditions and common experiences the group has which the new person cannot identify with.

Dr. Lyle Schaller makes an important contribution in understanding the process of incorporation. While people may be received into the *membership circle* of a church or Sunday School class, they do not automatically become members of the *fellowship circle*[21]—the members who feel a sense of belonging and who feel fully accepted into the fellowship of that group.

This concept has been illustrated by the following diagram:

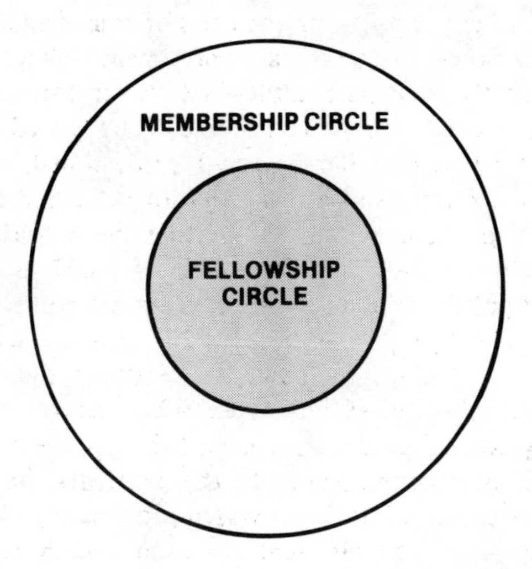


As might be expected, the people who drop out of church and Sunday School are almost always those in the outer circle who have not, for one reason or another, become members of the inner circle.

Remember, keeping Sunday School classes "open" to new people is a continuing job. It does not happen automatically.

5. *An effective Sunday School regularly establishes new groups and classes.* There are two simple, proven principles concerning the total number of classes in your Sunday School. They are: "merging existing groups inhibits growth," and "establishing new groups encourages growth." Both history and present research have proven these principles to be true.

In an article entitled "Sunday School, Small Groups, and Church Growth," Richard Myers describes his research in this area. Using two equally divided groups of ministers, each representing one church, the first group was told: if a Sunday School teacher in your church resigns this year, do not replace him or her. Instead combine that class with another class of about the same age to make one larger class. Keep a close watch on the attendance in the new class and record what happens."

A useful way to learn more about the "openness" and feeling of acceptance among the members of your Sunday School is a simple attitude survey. The questions below may be duplicated and completed anonymously by each person.

## PART A

DIRECTIONS: For each statement below, circle the number which most closely reflects your feelings. Note the description under the numbers one and five. If you strongly agree with one or the other, circle the "1" or the "5." If you feel less strongly about the statement, circle "2" or "4." If you don't feel one way or the other, circle "3." Please respond to each item, and be honest.

1. When I first joined this class I . . .

| **1** | **2** | **3** | **4** | **5** |
|---|---|---|---|---|
| had a hard time getting to know other members. | | | | found it quite easy to become part of the "gang." |

2. I presently feel that I "fit" in my Sunday School class like a . . .

| **1** | **2** | **3** | **4** | **5** |
|---|---|---|---|---|
| square peg in a round hole. | | | | hand in glove. |

3. The number of close friends I have in Sunday School is . . .

| **1** | **2** | **3** | **4** | **5** |
|---|---|---|---|---|
| 0-1 | 2-3 | 4-5 | 6-7 | 8+ |

4. I imagine if I were a typical visitor in my class I would . . .

| 1 | 2 | 3 | 4 | 5 |
|---|---|---|---|---|
| probably be ignored. | | | | be impressed with the friendliness of others toward me. |

5. When the class is over, members . . .

| 1 | 2 | 3 | 4 | 5 |
|---|---|---|---|---|
| talk only to other members. | | | | make it a point to introduce themselves to new people and get to know them. |

**PART B**

Answer the following questions either "yes" or "no."

A. I have a specific and regular duty in my church that I am responsible for (other than attending). **Yes** **No**

B. The subject of how our class welcomes new people has been discussed in the last two months. **Yes** **No**

C. If I were to invite a friend to my Sunday School class, I would feel apprehensive as to whether he or she might be ignored, or not feel welcomed by the group. **Yes** **No**

D. We have had a fairly large number of people visit the class whom I have not seen return. **Yes** **No**

As you analyze the results of this survey, look for the number of 1s and 2s that were circled in Part A. If there is a significant number, you have a problem and need to look for ways to solve it. In Part B, if a fairly large number of people answered "no" to the first two questions, or "yes" to the last two, you have a problem and will want to consider ways to solve it.

The second group of ministers was given a different set of instructions: "In every children's department with two or more classes, add another teacher and another class. Reassign the existing pupils to give all classes an equal enrollment. Monitor the growth patterns of these classes for the coming year."

In a year's time, dramatic changes had taken place in both groups. In the first group, attendance in every combined class had *declined* to the size of the original groups, resulting in decreased Sunday School attendance. This decrease was soon reflected in church membership also.

In the second group, just the opposite happened. By the end of the first year, all the classes that had been divided had grown back to the size of the original class, resulting in increased Sunday School attendance and a significant increase in church membership.

Myers notes:

> "The experiment provides a certain degree of evidence that the addition of classes may be an important variable to growth—Sunday School, as well as church, growth. Attendance in two classes will likely be larger than the attendance would have been with only one class. Eventual attendance in three classes should be larger than in just two. As the Sunday School provides the opportunity for more persons to be involved in meaningful growth programs, attendance grows."[22]

Eight good reasons tell us why new units should be established:

1) New units (classes, groups, organizations) provide a positive answer and response to human need.
2) New units are often more effective in incorporating people into a caring, belonging fellowship.
3) New units enlarge homogeneous appeal to new "kinds" of people.
4) New units are needed to replace those groups which have stagnated or have reached their saturation level.
5) New units provide Christians with meaningful involvement and service opportunities.
6) New units discourage clustered, self-serving attitudes and programs.

7) New units are usually more effective in winning new people to Christ and the church.
8) New units help the "single cell" church begin the process of cell multiplication and growth.

Myers' study, in addition to supporting the idea that new groups produce new growth, seems to verify two other principles of Sunday School growth mentioned earlier. First, most groups reach their maximum growth level in less than one year and seldom grow much more after that time. Second, Sunday School classes have a built-in growth ceiling, above which growth will not occur.

This same phenomenon is regularly seen in churches. When two churches merge, the marriage is based on the assumption that two sick "halves" will make a healthier "whole." This seldom happens.[23] Local churches planting new churches, however, discover that, far from depleting the resources of the mother church, the effort in planting new churches is repaid many times over in new enthusiasm and in increased ministry, involvement, and growth.[24]

Actually, many *small* churches are much more effective in reaching people than a few *large* churches. This has been shown in a number of research studies. One typical study done by Dr. Charles Chaney, Director of Church Extension for the Illinois Baptist State Association, showed that the newer and usually the smaller the church was, the greater proportion of baptisms and converts it had.[25] As a church grows older, the number of baptisms per hundred members usually drops markedly. Twenty churches of 50 members will normally baptize many more converts than two churches of 500, even though total membership in both groups is 1000. The same principle applies to small and large classes in the Sunday School.

These fascinating equations (new units = growth), (merger = decline), have a simple, yet important implication for congregations concerned with incorporating new believers: Sunday Schools that regularly start new classes regularly experience growth as a result.[26] Sunday Schools that merge classes, for whatever reason, usually find that the result is decline.

"How do you go about starting a new Sunday School class?" Here are nine simple steps:

**STEPS IN STARTING A NEW CLASS**

1. Define a target group of people you wish to reach.
2. Research the group and the kind of class that would meet their particular needs.
3. Find a committed lay person(s) willing to be involved in starting such a new class. The person should be similar to the target group.
4. Train this person in principles of starting a new group.
5. Begin the recruiting process prior to the first class session.
6. Find an appropriate meeting place and space.
7. Stress the importance of the first several months. They are critical to the success of the class.
8. Keep accurate records of the experience for reference in starting later classes.
9. Build in monitoring and evaluation procedures during the first nine months.

Who are your prospects for starting a new Sunday School class? You have three choices: present Sunday School members, church members not active in Sunday School, and those not involved in church or Sunday School.

Many Sunday Schools make the mistake of starting a new class by dividing an old one . . . taking present Sunday School members and putting them into new groups.[27] This is the least desirable choice of the three and may even frustrate growth through breaking up friendships and creating animosity. The key to successfully starting new Sunday School classes lies in reaching non-Sunday School members, both inside and outside of the local church.

Jeff Williams is a 33-year-old assistant manager of a life insurance company and an active member of his church; but, until recently, not a member of the Sunday School. At a recent church growth seminar we spoke with Jeff:

INTERVIEWER: You're a member of Grace United Methodist, here in El Paso. How long have you been a member?

JEFF WILLIAMS: Since 1968.

I: What do you think about the Sunday School?

JW: For a long time, I really didn't think that much of it. I guess I thought it was kind of Mickey Mouse.

I: So you were not an active Sunday School member. But now you are. What happened?

JW: A new class was starting and my wife and I decided to give it a try. We were invited by a person who told us it would be something we would really enjoy.

I: The class was made up of how many?

JW: I think there were five couples, although now we're up to 20 in only a four-month period.

I: What is your feeling of Sunday School now?

JW: Tremendous! It's a big part of my church life.

I: What does it do for you personally?

JW: It's the sharing with other people; it uplifts me. We are able to discuss and even debate from time to time. It's stimulating, exciting, and I look forward to it on Sunday morning as much as, if not more than, anything else.

I: How did the new couples, who were not initially involved, get into the group?

JW: We went to friends that we knew in the church, who were not involved in the Sunday School and invited them to come. For some of them it took three or four Sundays to get them there, but once they were part of us, they wanted to stay.

I: What is the future of the class?

JW: Very good. We are presently thinking about how to start another class, where we can invite other members, and—more importantly—non-members of the church.

This class was formed primarily with existing church members who were not part of the Sunday School. But as Jeff said, already the group is considering sponsoring a new class to reach others outside the church.

What about classes that include non-churched people in the community . . . a nut most Sunday School leaders think impossible to crack?

Pastor Joe Harding of the United Protestant Church in Richland, Washington, relates the experiences of his church in starting new groups:

> As we identify needs that people have, we form groups to meet these needs. So we're constantly forming new groups, new outposts. And people tell other people about that and they come through a new choir, a newcomers group, marriage enrichment, through marriage encounter, through parent effectiveness training, through this group or that. And then, as a result, they enroll in a pastor's seminar . . . just to learn. No obligation to join. But after they are in there seven weeks, over 90% end up becoming committed members of the church.[28]

Many Sunday Schools find that topically-oriented electives, which vary throughout the year, are an excellent way to reach people outside the church.

Rev. Jim Tait, of Arvada Covenant Church in Arvada, Colorado, has observed in his church that . . .

> Adult education has become the fastest growing area in our Sunday School. We are entering our third year of expanded adult electives and are able to offer a wide variety of classes using this system (24 total). This has been a start for us to really meet needs . . .[29]

## LEADERSHIP FOR NEW GROUPS

What about leaders in these new groups? Who starts them? Who is responsible for them?

The diagram below helps visualize an important strategy in successfully providing leadership for new groups. Your present Sunday School leadership base and the roles they perform look like this:

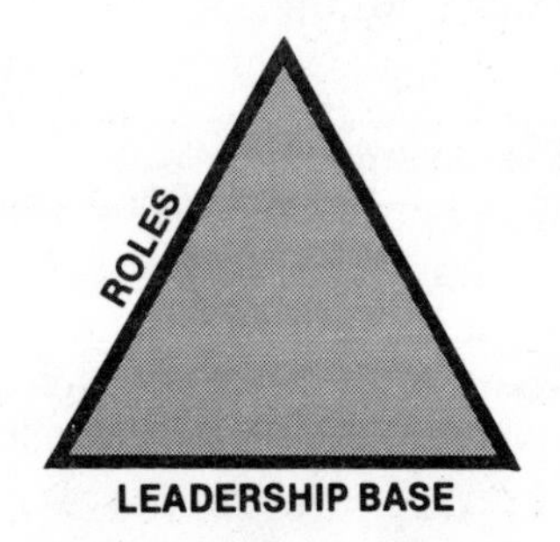

Starting new classes, using your existing base of leadership for these new responsibilities, is visualized below. The approach is to increase the responsibilities before increasing the leadership base:

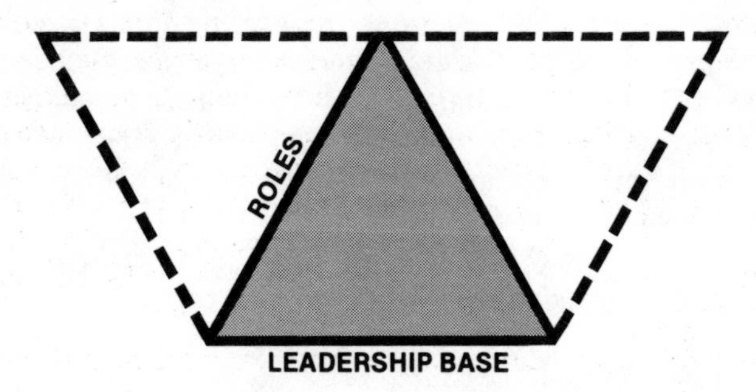


This strategy has three deficiencies. First, it puts a ceiling on the possible number of new groups that may be started, simply through lack of existing leaders. Second, it greatly increases the chance of present leaders becoming "burned out." Third, it reduces the number of roles available to other people in the Sunday School.

A more effective strategy for starting new groups is to increase the leadership base before increasing the responsibilities:

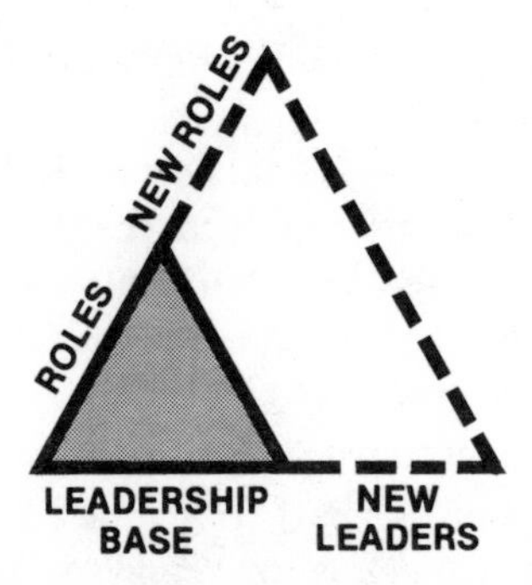


With this leadership strategy of starting new classes, growth can continue indefinitely.[30]

The First Baptist Church of Jackson, Mississippi, is an excellent example of the way creating new classes can turn a Sunday School growth curve straight up. In 1975, the church had one Sunday School session (9:40 - 10:20) which included 30 departments (of three to six classes each) and 180 Sunday School officers and teachers. Under the direction of Rev. David Roddy, Minister of Education, the Sunday School began to emphasize creating new units and enlarging the organizational structure. By the end of the next year, a second Sunday School session (11:00 - 12:00) had been started, and the number of departments had grown to 44, with a total of 210 teachers and officers. In an organization regularly creating new units, growth potential is multiplied enormously. The church, at this writing, has since added a third Sunday School hour, (8:20 - 9:30), and has grown to 62 departments, and has 364 officers and teachers.

We had the opportunity to chat with Rev. Roddy recently and learn more about the church's strategy.

INTERVIEWER: First Baptist has seen excellent Sunday School growth in the last six to eight years. Do you attribute this growth to your emphasis on starting new classes and departments?

RODDY: Yes, to a very large extent. I can tell you for sure that we didn't begin growing and then decide to add new classes. It was just the opposite situation. As we began to reorganize our Sunday School structure and begin a few new classes, growth followed just as day follows night.

I: How did you start the new classes?

R: I remember a typical case in 1977 when we first began to get serious about starting new classes. A few young couples in the church were going to be married around the same time. I told them, "Instead of getting you into an old class, let's start a new one." So we began a class for newly marrieds. By the end of the first year there were 65 class members and we now have 125.

I: So you build classes to reach similar kinds of people.

R: Yes, that's one of our basic principles. Just last November, in fact, we started a class for "single again" people who are now remarried. We began with four couples and the class now has 26 enrolled. But we also offer a wide variety of electives each quarter for people with special interests. So, electives are also an important part of our focus as we create new classes.

Many Sunday Schools that place a high priority on starting new classes have found it helpful to form a committee solely responsible for identifying possible areas in which to begin new classes. Such a committee helps the Sunday School creatively and continuously meet needs of members and potential new members. It also enables continued growth in the Sunday School when existing classes reach their natural plateaus. And it provides additional opportunities for role involvement by members—an essential part of any incorporation strategy.

Bill and Mary McKay could have been active, involved, enthusiastic members of their church right now. They could have been pioneers in a new class started for them and other couples in the church looking for a place to belong. But, for Bill and Mary, it is too late. If they are typical, research tells us they will not be back. In most cases they will not even try another church. They're gone.

Transforming new members into responsible church members is perhaps the most overlooked responsibility of the local church. The back doors of our churches are used much more frequently than most of us would like to admit. However, the Sunday School, when properly structured and monitored, is one of the most effective ways the local church has to close its back door and keep more Bills and Marys from becoming lost and forgotten statistics somewhere on the bottom of a basement file drawer.

## FOOTNOTES

### CHAPTER SIX

1. Lyle E. Schaller, *Hey, That's Our Church* (Nashville: Abingdon, 1975), p. 147.
2. C. Peter Wagner, lecture presented at LAMP Seminar, Pasadena, California.
3. "Lake Avenue Philosophy of Ministry" (Lake Avenue Congregational Church, Pasadena, California).
4. Warren J. Hartman, *Membership Trends: A Study of Decline and Growth in the United Methodist Church 1949 - 1975* (Nashville: Discipleship Resources, 1976), p. 41.
5. Flavil R. Yeakley, *Why Churches Grow* (Arvada, Colorado: Christian Communications, Inc., 1979), p. 54.

6. Warren J. Hartman, *A Study of the Church School in the United Methodist Church* (Nashville: Board of Education, 1972), p. 54.
7. Yeakley, op. cit. pp. 43-44.
8. C. Peter Wagner, *Our Kind of People* (Atlanta: John Knox Press, 1979), p. 76.
9. Ruth T. Doyle, and Sheila M. Kelly, "Comparison of Trends in Ten Denominations, 1950 - 1975" in *Understanding Church Growth and Decline 1950 - 1979,* ed. Dean R. Hoge and David A. Roozen (New York: Pilgrim Press, 1979), p. 156.
10. An excellent tool for identifying new prospects and monitoring the involvement level of new members is "The Caring System" kit available from Christian Communication, 150 S. Los Robles #600, Pasadena, California 91101.
11. John S. Savage, *The Apathetic and Bored Church Member* (Pittsford, New York: LEAD Consultants, 1976).
12. L. Ray Sells and Donald LaSuer, *The Caring System* (Pasadena: Christian Communication, 1979), p. 51.
13. George G. Hunter III, *The Contagious Congregation* (Nashville: Abingdon, 1979), p. 121.
14. Yeakley, op. cit. p. 35.
15. Ibid., p. 36.
16. Ibid.
17. Ibid., p. 37.
18. Jim Walter, "Using Growth Principles in Adult Outreach" in *Reaching Adults Through the Sunday School,* ed. Larry Shotwell (Nashville: Convention Press, 1979), p. 47.
19. E.S. Anderson, *The Sunday School Growth Spiral* (Nashville: Convention Press, 1978), p. 73.
20. C. Peter Wagner, lecture presented at LAMP Seminar, Pasadena, California.
21. Lyle E. Schaller, *Assimilating New Members* (Nashville: Abingdon, 1978), p. 69.
22. Richard A. Myers, "Sunday School, Small Groups, and Church Growth," CHURCH GROWTH: AMERICA 4, no. 4 (September/October, 1978), p. 8.
23. Edgar R. Trexler, *Creative Congregations* (Nashville: Abingdon, 1972), p. 104.
24. Charles L. Chaney and Ron S. Lewis, *Design for Church Growth* (Nashville: Broadman, 1977), p. 144.
25. Charles L. Chaney, "How To Create A Climate for Church Planting" CHURCH GROWTH: AMERICA 5, no. 3 (Summer, 1979), p. 6.
26. Walter, op. cit., p. 48.
27. Schaller, op. cit., p. 102.
28. From the film, *But, I'm Just A Layman!* (Pasadena, Ca.: Christian Communication, 1979).
29. "Adult Education in the Learning Church" THE COVENANT COMPANION 69, no. 2 (January 15, 1980), p. 5.
30. For a more thorough discussion of this concept, see David A. Womack, *The Pyramid Principle* (Minneapolis: Bethany Press, 1977).

# GROWTH: TRAINING FOR EFFECTIVE WITNESS

**The study of the Bible enables Christians to know the will of God for their lives, for their church, and for their world.**

**The Sunday School trains and equips Christians to do the work of the Church.**

**The Sunday School can be most effective in training Christians to win others to Christ and help make churches grow.**

These three truths are the basic foundation on which the Sunday School should train its members.

The Bible gives clear testimony that all men and women, boys and girls should have the opportunity to know Jesus Christ, and to accept Him as their Savior in the fellowship of His Church. Romans 16:25-27 tells us that the gospel itself was revealed by command of the Eternal God "to bring all peoples of the earth to faith and obedience." Matthew records that Jesus commanded His followers "to disciple *panta ta ethne,*" i.e., all the peoples of the earth. Since no one can become a disciple of Jesus Christ without repenting of his sins, being baptized, and becoming a responsible member of Christ's Body—the Church—it is apparent that discipling the peoples of earth requires a vast multiplication of sound, healthy churches.

The Bible also gives clear testimony that all Christians are witnesses. Telling others of Christ is a normal duty and potentially a great pleasure for all Christians. In the United States live approximately 60 million practicing Christians. Beyond them are at least 160 million Americans who are "Christians" in name only or persons with no Christian faith at all—humanists, secularists, rationalists, hedonists, Marxists, materialists or, in a word, pagans. All these "others" need to be creatively confronted with an opportunity to meet and receive Jesus Christ. According to a recent study, over half of these "pagans" could see themselves as active church members and would be open to an invitation from the church community.[1]

Beyond the United States live hundreds of millions of girls and boys, women and men who know practically nothing of God's one way of salvation. Most have never even heard the Gospel. Becoming a Christian has never been a option. Yet, the Bible is crystal clear that *all these* are to hear the gospel. As recorded in Mark 16:15, the risen Lord commanded His followers "to go into all the world and preach the Gospel to the whole creation. He who believes and is baptized will be saved; he who does not believe will be condemned." The Bible leaves no room for excuses: every Christian should feel a responsibility to give these people a real chance to hear, believe, and live. Such witnessing, both at home and abroad, means a mighty, ongoing discipling of all peoples—a never-ceasing growth of the Church, a continuous multiplying of cells of redeemed congregations of Christians.

## WILLING BUT UNTRAINED

Good Christians, the backbone of our churches, thoroughly agree with the previous paragraphs. Those millions who have yet to believe ought to hear the Gospel, ought to be discipled, ought to become responsible members of churches of Jesus Christ. Certainly! But nevertheless, most Christians seldom speak to others about the Savior. "I'd like to," many say. "I know I am a witness, but I have never done it." "I feel awkward." "I'd much rather the pastor do it, he's hired to do such things."

"I was not taught how to do it." "I wouldn't know what to say."

A faithful lay person once said to me, "I'm ready to spend an evening a week calling; but beyond inviting people to come to our church, I don't know what to say. I wish our Bible School had classes in effective Christian witnessing. I think quite a number of us would enroll."

Pastor James Kennedy of Coral Ridge Presbyterian Church in Ft. Lauderdale, Florida, found that when, from the pulpit, he exhorted his people to go out and evangelize, they did so . . . once! Not knowing what to say, how to pass from opening remarks on the weather to talking about Christ and His way of life or how to answer objections, they had such a thin or even unpleasant experience that they did not go out again. They felt such witnessing got nowhere. Then Kennedy himself learned how to present Christ and talk about spiritual matters naturally and easily. He taught the willing, eager, but untrained Christians how to be creative, effective witnesses. His congregation has grown enormously as a result.

## TRAINING PASTORS IS NOT ENOUGH

Dr. Win Arn and Dr. Peter Wagner have trained thousands of pastors in church growth. During seminary classes and growth seminars, professional clergymen learn much about church growth. The Church in America is starting to come alive to church growth. Leaders are increasingly supporting it. Entire denominations are setting growth goals. Individual congregations are waking to growth, increasing their memberships, developing challenging growth strategy, and planting daughter churches. Church growth is becoming a major agenda item for nearly every denomination in the country. This is encouraging—but it is ***not enough!***

The facts are becoming increasingly clear that local churches grow when ordinary Christians carry the good news into their multitudinous circles of factories, ski clubs, PTAs, neighborhoods, new housing developments, apartments, businessmen's clubs, university gatherings, lumber camps . . . where people reach people. To date, not many ordinary, earnest Christians are *out there* witnessing charmingly, persuasively, and convincingly. Nor will they be, until the Sunday Schools of America begin teaching hundreds of thousands of their lay people how to be normal, effective advocates of Christ and their church.

## AN ESSENTIAL PART OF THE SUNDAY SCHOOL

The Study of the Bible enables Christians to know the will of God for their lives, their church, and their world. It is clearly God's will that all people hear the Gospel and have a chance to believe and be saved.

Without the study of the Bible, Christians would never know this. Bible study in Sunday Schools ought to teach Christians, at all levels, of God's will in regard to the evangelization of both neighbors and "all peoples."

The Sunday School prepares Christians to do the work of the Church. God expects, and has directly commissioned, the Church to propagate the Gospel, to bring people to repentance and belief on Christ, and encourage them to become reliable members of the Household of God. *This is a most important work of the Church.* Hence, the Sunday School rightfully prepares Christians for effective witness. Classes should regularly learn about God's will in evangelization, about effective ways of presenting the Gospel, about courteous, persuasive witnessing.

Classes should investigate how university faculties will respond to various types of witness different from factory workers or first generation immigrants; how "tired" Christians, the bored and apathetic, can be encouraged into new vitality; how pagans born of pagans should be approached. These strategies can be learned. And they are immensely important in effective evangelism. There is no better place to learn them than the Sunday School class.

## SUBJECTS FOR STUDY

A class should study how, from 120 frightened believers on the day before Pentecost, the church grew mightily—to 3120 on Pentecost, to 5000 men, plus women and children, in a few weeks. How the Lord added *daily* those who were believing and being saved. How Christians spoke the Word with boldness and believers were added to the Lord. How the Word of God increased and the numbers of the disciples multiplied greatly.

An interesting and fruitful study is how many of the Levites, a closed caste, became obedient to the faith. Or how, when persecution broke out and all Christians were scattered through the hill country of Judea and Samaria, the refugees enthusiastically told the people about their joy in Christ—so great that even being driven out of their homes did not dampen their ardor.

The study of the book of Acts, to learn what it teaches about normal contagious witness, ought to be a regular part of every Sunday School curriculum. The New Testament records how Christians, at first, told only Jews of the Messiah. But the news was so good that in Caesarea, Samaria, and Antioch, it broke over into other kinds of people—Roman soldiers, Greek-speaking Syrians, and Samaritans. Social barriers crumbled before the contagious witness of Christians enthusiastic about their new-found faith. Learners, both young and old, must catch the excitement these early Christians displayed in sharing Christ with people of varying backgrounds.

Many Church Schools should also include classes on effective contemporary witness, in which the members study the strengths and weaknesses of various means of outreach. Dr. James Kennedy's *Evangelism Explosion*[2] is a well-thought-out plan which could become the subject of study and practice for a quarter. Other books on growth and effective outreach should be texts for study. Hunter's book *The Contagious Congregation*[3] is one; Wagner's *Your Church Can Grow*[4] is excellent; so are Arn and McGavran's *Ten Steps for Church Growth*[5], *How to Grow A Church,*[6] and *Back to Basics in Church Growth.*[7] *Understanding Church Growth*[8] is the basic text in church growth. It is a book which serious students of church growth will want to master.

Other topics to be studied for a quarter might include:

- Great biblical themes of redemption
- Historical study of the growth of Christianity
- Our church's growth potential
- Contemporary methods of evangelism
- How to share your faith
- Spiritual gifts and the growth of the Body
- Strategies, tactics, and tools for growth
- Research on the growth (and decline?) of our congregation
- Training new members and new converts for outreach
- Building bridges to unreached people in the community

Many systems of presenting Christ and His claims are being used today. Churches wishing to build growth thinking into the Sunday School should study a variety of options and encourage the ones that best fit the church's understanding of the faith, the church members, and the opportunities to obey their Lord in discipling men and women in their sphere of influence. Some approaches will, of course, work better for certain congregations and denominations than for others.

One excellent emerging source of growth-oriented Sunday School courses is the Institute for American Church Growth.[9] In addition to several seminars for pastors and Sunday School leaders, the organization is publishing adult Sunday School courses which build in the underlying foundations necessary for developing a "growth conscience" and growth expertise. The Institute also offers material by which the pastor can conduct an excellent teacher-oriented seminar, including a variety of

**WHY "GROWTH-CENTERED" CLASSES SHOULD HAVE A MAJOR PLACE IN EVERY SUNDAY SCHOOL**

1. To obey God's command to "Go . . . and make disciples."
2. To help the laity find and use their gifts.
3. To enable members to find personal meaning and ministry.
4. To reach lost people and bring them home.
5. To bring the chief goal of the Sunday School in line with the chief goal of the church—making disciples.
6. To provide necessary training to many persons in the church.
7. To develop competency in young people for effective evangelism.
8. To enable new members and new converts to reach their friends.

learning activities for participants. The seminar helps teachers and leaders (1) better understand the priorities of the Sunday School and (2) develop practical ways to begin a growth pattern.

## A CONTAGIOUS WITNESS

At a small church where I recently worshipped, one of the children, who was known by the whole congregation, needed to have a serious operation. People in the church were asked to pray on the day of the operation. One man, at noon on the day of the operation, told the other men with whom he worked of the need for prayer. A number of them asked to join him in prayer for the child they had never met. The church member discovered that he was working with several ardent Christians and several who wanted to be. As a result, a Bible study group at that place of work was formed and through it three came to Christian faith. Spontaneous, unplanned witness—*the overflow of the joyous heart*—cannot be programmed. It is a normal result of Christian living.[10] Such contagious incidents are expected and encouraged in Sunday School classes as a means of carrying out the Great Commission.

The power of the Sunday School to create a corps of intelligent, charming, contagious, and persuasive witnesses, can only be described as awesome. We must pray and work toward the goal of multiplying such classes; we need thousands of them. It is not an easy task. Christian educators should demand the creation of such biblical courses on witnessing. Christian publishers, sensing the urgency of recapturing the initiative in evangelism, should publish new courses. Authors of conviction and experience in evangelism and church growth should write quarterlies and courses. Pastors and Sunday School superintendents should begin the new courses and see that suitable classes are available and enrollment encouraged. Finally, the conviction should spread that men and women, boys and girls without Christ and the Bible are really lost; and with Him they are a new creation. Without that conviction, nothing will happen. With it, the Church School will greatly multiply.

If each pastor were supported in this new vision of training for growth, and if classes of adults, young adults, collegians, and high schoolers busily studied and practiced evangelism/

church growth, what an army would soon be ready for deployment! What a different audience the pastor would be preaching to at eleven thirty! How many new ideas and better approaches would be born as class after class studied and learned of God's will and asked, "What does God want *us* to do in our particular circumstances?"

A time of great flowering lies ahead for those churches whose Sunday Schools systematically teach God's will in evangelism and give abundant opportunity to carry it out.

## FOOTNOTES

### CHAPTER SEVEN

1. George Gallup, "The Unchurched American" (March/April 1979) CHURCH GROWTH: AMERICA 5, no. 2, p. 9.
2. D. James Kennedy, *Evangelism Explosion* (Wheaton: Tyndale, 1977).
3. George G. Hunter, *The Contagious Congregation* (Nashville: Abingdon, 1979).
4. C. Peter Wagner, *Your Church Can Grow* (Glendale: Regal, 1976).
5. Donald A. McGavran & Winfield C. Arn, *Ten Steps for Church Growth* (New York: Harper & Row, 1977).
6. Donald A. McGavran & Winfield C. Arn, *How To Grow A Church* (Glendale: Regal, 1973).
7. Donald A. McGavran & Winfield C. Arn, *Back to Basics in Church Growth* (Wheaton:Tyndale, 1980).
8. Donald A. McGavran, *Understanding Church Growth* (2nd edition Grand Rapids: Eerdmans, 1980).
9. A free catalog of church growth resources and Sunday School curriculum is available from the *Institute for American Church Growth,* (150 S. Los Robles, #600, Pasadena, CA 91101). Also, investigate the growth-oriented curriculum available from denominational or other curriculum publishers.
10. Tom Wolf, "Oikos Evangelism" (January/February 1978), 4, no. 1, p. 13.

CHAPTER EIGHT

# GROWTH: THE GIFT FOR TEACHING

What if your Sunday School superintendent opened the next teachers' meeting by saying: "We are encouraging those of you who feel you do not have the gift of teaching to think about other areas of service in the church you might enjoy. We feel it would be better for you and for the Sunday School if you did not continue teaching next quarter."

What would be the reactions to such a pronouncement? They might vary from "The Sunday School is doomed!" to "Hallelujah, I'm free!" to "How am I supposed to know if I have the gift of teaching?!"

Studying, searching for, discovering, and using one's spiritual gifts are becoming increasing concerns of Christians in the 1980s.[1] Christians who have found and are using their spiritual gifts have discovered that (a) they are more productive and joyous in their Christian life, and (b) their participation in church roles and responsibilities is substantially more rewarding.

It is a liberating insight to realize that God does not expect all things of all people—no, not even Sunday School teachers! For many it is like a heavy load loosened from their backs to learn that some Christians are gifted for teaching and others are not; and that God does not expect Christians without such a gift to spend hours upon frustrating hours doing what they neither enjoy nor are very good at.

## SPIRITUAL GIFTS—AN OVERVIEW

The interest, insights, and understandings in spiritual gifts are relatively new. Three out of every four books on the subject have been written since 1970. The first 16mm color film, *Discover Your Gifts,*[2] was recently produced on the subject. Numerous denominations, as well as local churches, are now looking seriously at the implications spiritual gifts may have for them.

Yet the concept of spiritual gifts is actually as old as the New Testament. Peter notes that each Christian has been given a gift (I Peter 4:10). Paul says, "Now concerning spiritual gifts, brethren, I do not want you to be uninformed" (I Cor. 12:1). Numerous other passages throughout the Bible refer directly or indirectly to the fact that Christians are given gifts to use in Christ's service.

What are "spiritual gifts"? A commonly accepted definition of a spiritual gift is ". . . a special attribute given by the Holy Spirit to every member of the Body of Christ, according to God's grace, within the context of the Body."[3]

Throughout the New Testament, and particularly in three specific chapters, spiritual gifts are named. If you do some research yourself, you will find the following list of gifts from these three passages:

From *Romans 12*: Prophecy, Service, Teaching, Exhortation, Giving, Leadership, Mercy;

From *I Corinthians 12* (in addition to the list given in Romans): Wisdom, Knowledge, Faith, Healing, Miracles, Discernment, Tongues, Interpretation of Tongues, Apostle, Helps, Administration;

From *Ephesians 4* (in addition to those already listed): Evangelist, Pastor.

## WHAT ARE THE SPIRITUAL GIFTS?

Not all authors agree on all gifts. Other authorities believe, with some justification, that there may be more spiritual gifts than are mentioned in the New Testament. But here is a beginning.[4]

**A. Prophecy.** The gift of prophecy is the special ability that God gives to certain members of the Body of Christ to receive and communicate an immediate message of God to His people. *I Cor. 12:10, 28; Rom. 12:6, Eph. 4:11, Acts 15:32; Acts 21:9-11; Luke 7:26.*

**B. Pastor.** The gift of pastor is the special ability that God gives to certain members of the Body of Christ to assume a long-term personal responsibility for the spiritual welfare of a group of believers. *Eph. 4:11; I Tim. 3:1-7; John 10:1-18; I Pet. 5:1-3.*

**C. Teaching.** The gift of teaching is the special ability that God gives to certain members of the Body of Christ to communicate information relevant to the health and ministry of the Body and its members in such a way that others will learn. *I Cor. 12:28; Rom. 12:7; Eph. 4:11-14; Acts 18:24-28; Acts 20:20-21.*

**D. Wisdom.** The gift of wisdom is the special ability that God gives to certain members of the Body of Christ to know the mind of the Holy Spirit in such a way as to receive insight into how given knowledge may best be applied to specific needs arising in the Body of Christ. *I Cor. 12:8; Acts 6:3, 10; II Pet. 3:15; I Cor. 2:1-13; James 1:5-6.*

**E. Knowledge.** The gift of knowledge is the special ability that God gives to certain members of the Body of Christ to discover, accumulate, analyze and clarify information and ideas which are pertinent to the growth and well-being of the Body. *I Cor. 12:8; Acts 5:1-11; I Cor. 2:14; Col. 2:2-3*

**F. Exhortation.** The gift of exhortation is the special ability that God gives to certain members of the Body of Christ to minister words of comfort, consolation, encouragement and counsel to other members of the Body in such a way that they feel helped and healed. *Rom. 12:8; I Tim. 4:13; Heb. 10:25; Acts 14:22.*

**G. Discerning of Spirits.** The gift of discerning of spirits is the special ability that God gives to certain members of the Body of Christ to know with assurance whether certain behavior purported to be of God is in reality divine, human or Satanic. *I Cor. 12:10; Acts 16:16-18; I John 4:1-6*

**H. Giving.** The gift of giving is the special ability that God gives to certain members of the Body of Christ to contribute their material resources to the work of the Lord with liberality and cheerfulness. *Rom. 12:8; II Cor. 8:1-7; II Cor. 9:2, 6-8*

**I. Helps.** The gift of helps is the special ability that God gives to certain members of the Body of Christ to invest the talents they have in life and the ministry of other members of the Body, thus enabling them to increase the effectiveness of their own spiritual gifts. *I Cor. 12:28; Rom. 16:1-2; Acts 9:36*

**J. Mercy.** The gift of mercy is the special ability that God gives to certain members of the Body of Christ to feel genuine empathy and compassion for individuals, both Christian and non-Christian, who suffer distressing physical, mental or emotional problems, and to translate that compassion into cheerfully-done deeds which reflect Christ's love and alleviate the suffering. *Rom. 12:8; Acts 16:33-34; Luke 10:33-35; Mark 9:41*

**K. Missionary.** The gift of missionary is the special ability that God gives to certain members of the Body of Christ to minister whatever other spiritual gifts they have in a second culture. *I Cor. 9:19-23; Acts 22:21; Acts 13:2, 3; Acts 8:4; Rom. 10:15*

**L. Evangelist.** The gift of the evangelist is the special ability that God gives to certain members of the Body of Christ to share the Gospel with unbelievers in such a way that men and women become Jesus' disciples and responsible members of the Body of Christ. *Eph. 4:11; Acts 8:5-6; Acts 8:26-40; II Tim. 4:5; Acts 21:8; Acts 14:21*

**M. Hospitality.** The gift of hospitality is the special ability that God gives to certain members of the Body of Christ to provide open house and warm welcome for those in need of food and lodging. *Rom. 12:9-13; Heb. 13:1-2; Acts 16:15; Rom. 16:23*

**N. Faith.** The gift of faith is the special ability that God gives to certain members of the Body of Christ to discern with extraordinary confidence the will and purposes of God for the future of His work. *I Cor. 12:9; Acts 27:21-25; Acts 11:22-24; Rom. 4:18-21; Heb. 11*

**O. Leadership.** The gift of leadership is the special ability that God gives to certain members of the Body of Christ to set goals in accordance with God's purpose for the future and to communicate these goals to others in such a way that they voluntarily and harmoniously work together to accomplish those goals for the glory of God. *Rom 12:8; Acts 15:7-11; I Tim. 5:17; Acts 7:10; Heb. 13:17*

**P. Administration.** The gift of administration is the special ability that God gives to certain members of the Body of Christ to understand clearly the immediate and long-range goals of a particular unit of the Body of Christ and to devise and execute effective plans for the accomplishment of those goals. *I Cor. 12:28; Acts 27:11; Acts 6:1-7*

**Q. Miracles.** The gift of miracles is the special ability that God gives to certain members of the Body of Christ to serve as human intermediaries through whom it pleases God to perform powerful acts that are perceived by observers to have altered the ordinary course of nature. *I Cor. 12:10, 28; Acts 19:11-20; Rom 15:18-19; Acts 9:36-42*

**R. Healing.** The gift of healing is the special ability that God gives to certain members of the Body of Christ to serve as human intermediaries through whom it pleases God to cure illness and restore health apart from the use of natural means. *I Cor. 12:9, 28; Acts 3:1-10; Acts 5:12-16; Acts 9:32-35*

**S. Tongues.** The gift of tongues is the special ability that God gives to certain members of the Body of Christ (a) to speak to God in a language they have never learned and/or (b) to receive and communicate an immediate message of God to his people through a divinely-anointed utterance in a language they have never learned. *I Cor. 12:10, 28; I Cor. 14:13-19; Acts 2:1-13; Acts 19:1-7; Acts 10:44-46*

**T. Interpretation.** The gift of interpretation is the special ability that God gives to certain members of the Body of Christ to make known in the vernacular the message of one who speaks in tongues. *I Cor. 12:10, 30; I Cor. 14:13, 26-28*

**U. Apostle.** The gift of apostle is the special ability that God gives to certain members of the Body of Christ to assume and exercise general leadership over a number of churches with an extraordinary authority in spiritual matters which is spontaneously recognized and appreciated by those churches. *I Cor. 12:28; Eph. 4:11; II Cor. 12:12; Eph. 3:1-9*

**V. Celibacy.** The gift of celibacy is the special ability that God gives to certain members of the Body of Christ to remain single and enjoy it; to be unmarried and not suffer undue sexual temptations. *I Cor. 7:7-8; Matt. 19:10-12*

**W. Intercession.** The gift of intercession is the special ability that God gives to certain members of the Body of Christ to pray for extended periods of time on a regular basis and to see frequent and specific answers to their prayers to a degree much greater than that which is expected of the average Christian. *James 5:14-16; I Tim. 2:1-2; Col. 1:9-12*

**X. Martyrdom.** The gift of martyrdom is the special ability that God gives to certain members of the Body of Christ to undergo suffering for the faith even to the point of death, while consistently displaying a joyous and victorious attitude which brings glory to God. *I Cor. 13:3; Acts 7:54-60; Acts 12: 1-5; Acts 8:1-4*

**Y. Service.** The gift of service is the special ability that God gives to certain members of the Body of Christ to identify the unmet needs involved in a task related to God's work, and to make use of available resources to meet those needs and help accomplish the desired goals. *Rom. 12:7; Acts 6:1-7; II Tim. 1:16-18*

## THE SUNDAY SCHOOL AND THE GIFT OF TEACHING

The New Testament often refers to the importance of teaching and the gift of teaching. This gift appears in all three of the major passages on spiritual gifts. As the apostles spread the Gospel and the early church grew with explosive vitality, the teaching gift is mentioned frequently. Acts records that new Christians were continually devoting themselves to the apostles' teaching (2:42). Paul refers to his own gift of teaching (II Tim. 1:11), and Acts records that he *taught* for an entire year at Antioch (11:26), for a year and a half at Corinth (18:11), and for two years at Ephesus (19:10). Teaching had a large part in the activity and growth of the early church, and rightly so.

Wagner defines the gift of teaching as: "The special ability God gives to certain members of the Body to communicate information relevant to the spiritual growth of members and numerical growth of the Body, in such a way that others will learn."[5]

Did you catch the important phrase? "to communicate . . . so others will learn."

Yet, what complicated requirements we often put on teachers

to fulfill the role of "teacher." Teachers are asked not only to teach a class, but to worry about planning, administration, follow-up, visitation, counseling, evangelism, recruitment. No wonder teachers are becoming harder and harder to find . . . Werning thinks they may all be collapsing from exhaustion![6]

Let's take a look at a Sunday School that applies the resources of its members on the basis of the spiritual gifts, rather than the requirements of the organization.

Those with the gift of teaching are responsible for preparing and presenting the lesson every Sunday. Teaching is essentially all they do. Some may be on the curriculum planning committee, but only in an advisory role. Teachers' time is spent primarily in study and lesson preparation. They are not expected to visit inactive members, keep rolls, complete reports, recruit new members; these concerns are delegated to others with more appropriate gifts. The teachers' concern and major responsibility in the church is teaching that class.

In such a Sunday School, the superintendent is seldom an ex-teacher. Perhaps he tried teaching a class once, but discovered he did not have the gift. The superintendent's gift, or the Director of Christian Education's gift, might be apostle and/or leader. The assistant superintendent would have the gift of administration.

The Christian education board is composed not of people who happen to be available, but of those who have various gifts which would relate to leading the Sunday School forward in growth. Such gifts as wisdom, faith, exhortation, discernment, administration and leadership should certainly be represented.

In a Sunday School using spiritual gifts, other activities and responsibilities that contribute to growth are delegated to appropriately gifted members. A strategy of reaching newcomers just moving into the community, for example, would easily utilize existing gifts. The gifts of service, giving, evangelism, mercy, wisdom, and helps would be creatively involved. Wagner points out that the gift of hospitality is mentioned in the Bible.[7] This gift is particularly effective when identified and deliberately structured into the activity of the Sunday School.

In many growing Sunday School classes, an individual or group is responsible for the incorporation of new people. Such people are concerned with monitoring involvement patterns of new members, and making a point of helping the newcomer become assimilated into the life of the group. Gifts such as exhortation, service, mercy, helps, intercession, pastor, and healing would often be exercised in carrying out this task.

For planning and implementing special growth-oriented events in the Sunday School, members with the gifts of service, helps, and administration are valuable. A special group in the class responsible for visiting sick or bereaved members should certainly have the gift of mercy, and perhaps the gifts of faith and exhortation. Christians responsible for visiting non-Christian prospects should definitely have the gift of evangelism. And for coordinating the efficient use of these gifts and people, people with the gift of administration and helps would be required.

## DISCOVERING YOUR SPIRITUAL GIFT

How do you find out what your spiritual gift is? And how do you help others discover their gifts? Wagner believes there are first several "prerequisites" which must be considered before one can begin searching for his or her spiritual gift:[8]

A) *You must be a Christian.* God reserves the gifts of the Holy Spirit for the members of His Body . . . those who have a personal relationship and commitment to Jesus Christ.

B) *You must believe you are gifted.* The Bible teaches that "Each one is given the manifestation of the Spirit for the common good" (I Cor. 12:7).

C) *You must want to discover your gift.* It means work, study, prayer, and commitment.

Most writers and authorities on the subject generally concur as to the process of discovering one's spiritual gift(s). Here are six steps which synthesize these writings, with special attention given to the gift of teaching.

*1. Pray.* Ask God for understanding and wisdom about spiritual gifts, and for direction in discovering your own gift. Thank Him for His grace in giving you gifts and dedicate your search for, and use of, your gifts to His honor. Commit yourself and your unique gifts to the growth of His church.

*2. Study.* Read books, study the gifts passages in the Bible, know what gifts God has given to His Body, and how they

## SPIRITUAL GIFTS IN THE SUNDAY SCHOOL—AN EXERCISE

In Column "A" are a variety of spiritual gifts. In Column "B" are descriptions of various activities that are performed in many growing Sunday Schools. Place the number of each activity in the blank in front of the spiritual gift which would complement the activity or role. (Refer to the list and descriptions of the various spiritual gifts on the previous pages if necessary).

**A**

a. ____ Service

b. ____ Teaching

c. ____ Exhortation

d. ____ Giving

e. ____ Leadership

f. ____ Mercy

g. ____ Wisdom

h. ____ Knowledge

i. ____ Faith

j. ____ Hospitality

k. ____ Missionary

l. ____ Apostle

m. ____ Helps

**B**

1. Inviting Sunday School prospects over for dinner and friendly visits.
2. Visiting non-Christian prospects.
3. Pray for Sunday School prospects and leaders/teachers.
4. Identifying areas of need within the community and suggesting ways the Sunday School could respond.
5. Visiting sick or bereaved Sunday School members.
6. Presenting a special message on the important role of each person in the Sunday School.
7. Leading a class study session of Acts and the growth of the early church.
8. Setting numerical goals for the Sunday School.

n. ____ Administration

o. ____ Evangelist

p. ____ Pastor

q. ____ Intercession

9. Endeavoring to keep all classes working toward the same goal.
10. Financially supporting a special Sunday School outreach project.
11. Seeking God's will in new areas of growth and ministry in the Sunday School.
12. Spearheading the starting of a new Sunday School class for a certain ethnic group in the community.
13. Counseling Sunday School leaders prior to decision-making meetings.
14. Serving as a spiritual "shepherd" of a class.
15. Assisting in any area where additional personnel are required.
16. Chairing a committee on reaching new people.
17. Researching information for a teacher in lesson preparation.

**Key:** a—4; b—7; c—6; d—10; e—8; f—5; g—13; h—17; i—11; j—1; k—12; l—9; m—15; n—16; o—2; p—14; q—3.

manifest themselves. Concerning the gift of teaching, talk with and observe people who have the gift and are using it. Ask them how they discovered their gift and what reinforcing events contributed to their discovery.

*3. Experiment.* Look around your church and endeavor to identify areas of need. Examine your concerns, remembering that many are gifted in areas for which they have a particular concern. Then experiment. If you are especially concerned about the growth and effectiveness of your Sunday School and the spiritual growth of Christians, the teaching gift may be a good one to investigate first.

*4. Question.* What degree of satisfaction do you feel in the areas you are experimenting with? How do you feel about it? Positive feelings usually evidence fulfillment and are a clue in discovering one's gift. Negative feelings may indicate your gifts are elsewhere. Do you enjoy teaching? Does it give you an inner sense of satisfaction to study, prepare, and present the lesson?

*5. Evaluate.* Are there positive results? Spiritual gifts are task-oriented . . . they are given for practical use in the Body of Christ. Do students in your class enjoy the lesson? Do they return? Are class members learning and growing? Are you, as a teacher, growing in confidence? Are additional opportunities opening for you to use your teaching gift? Are your efforts producing results? These questions, when truthfully answered, give clues and direction.

*6. Verify.* Look for confirmation from the Body. Do other Christians affirm your own ideas of what your gifts are? If not, you should re-evaluate your thinking. If students stay away from your classes or don't seem to be learning, your gift may be something other than teaching.

## FINDING THE GIFTED TEACHERS

The fact is that your Sunday School should not have teachers who do not have the gift of teaching. How, then do you find members with the gift of teaching?

To begin with, *teachers are not recruited.* Every willing member, and especially every new member, should work through a "Spiritual Gifts Discovery Program." Such a program is usually designed by church leaders in accordance with the church's philosophy of spiritual gifts. It may include a survey asking questions about personal abilities, interests, attitudes, preferences, and convictions of the member.[9] A take-home self study packet is provided, including books, Bible references, homework assignments, etc.[10] One or more experienced lay or staff persons conduct a personal interview with the individual. Discussion would center around past areas of service that have been personally rewarding and successful, special interests and skills of the member, the person's own analysis of his or her spiritual gift(s), and how he or she believes they might be used.

As part of the "Spiritual Gifts Discovery Program," a tentative "gifts profile" is then developed and discussed with the person. In it, potential gifts and areas of strength are noted and tentatively matched with specific tasks or roles available in the church. A strategy is then mapped out, with the member, on how to begin the process of verifying his or her gifts and then using and developing them in the church.

Church members who seem to be gifted in teaching are asked if they would like to sit in with a class of their particular interest and assist the present teacher. The Sunday School teacher is asked to work with the member in helping to nurture the newly-discovered gift of teaching. Over a period of months various responsibilities in teaching the class are given to the potential new teacher. If the experiences are good, if the person is enjoying a sense of fulfillment, and if there is positive reinforcement from the class, the new member is asked if he or she would like to consider starting a new class, as a new teacher.

## USING YOUR GIFT

Particularly in adult Sunday School classes, a teacher has the responsibility of teaching about spiritual gifts and helping the members discover their gifts.[11] The teacher should also stress that God gives gifts to use in serving others, not simply as a means of personal fulfillment. The discovery and use of spiritual gifts should be seen as a means to an end, not an end in itself. The use of these gifts must fit into the Sunday School's

## A TEACHING GIFT INVENTORY

The following questions will help you begin thinking about the spiritual gift of teacher. Whether you are or are not a teacher, you will enjoy answering the questions below and examining your own feelings. There will be, of course, other important indicators of what your gifts are; but here is a beginning.

Circle the number below each question which most closely approximates your response. You would circle "5", for example, if your answer was "always;" "4" if you would answer "usually;" "3" if you "occasionally" feel that way; "2" if you "seldom" can identify with the question; and "1" if your response is "never."

After you have completed your responses, add the total. If the number totals 100 or more, you may be gifted in the area of teaching. If your total was between 85 and 100 you should continue to investigate the gift of teaching as perhaps one of your secondary gifts.

Do you see yourself as a person able to help others learn and apply Biblical truths?

NEVER 1 2 3 4 5 ALWAYS

Do you view the Scriptures as a source of numerous insights which can be communicated to others?

NEVER 1 2 3 4 5 ALWAYS

Do you enjoy talking about spiritual truths, and their application, with others?

NEVER 1 2 3 4 5 ALWAYS

Do you enjoy researching and relating biblical concepts which influence other people's knowledge, attitudes, and behavior?

NEVER 1 2 3 4 5 ALWAYS

Do you find that enabling other Christians to be more obedient disciples is rewarding?

NEVER 1 2 3 4 5 ALWAYS

Do people ever say to you something like, "What you said the other day really helped me"?

NEVER 1 2 3 4 5 ALWAYS

Do you find it easy to organize a logical sequence of concepts or thoughts to communicate an idea?

NEVER 1 2 3 4 5 ALWAYS

Do you enjoy working with details?

NEVER 1 2 3 4 5 ALWAYS

Do you find that you can "practice what you preach"?

NEVER 1 2 3 4 5 ALWAYS

Do you like to tell stories and use various ways to make a point?

NEVER 1 2 3 4 5 ALWAYS

Do you see yourself as being patient with people?

NEVER 1 2 3 4 5 ALWAYS

Do people feel free to ask you questions without feeling "put down" or embarassed?

NEVER 1 2 3 4 5 ALWAYS

Are you able to accept criticism of your teaching?

NEVER 1 2 3 4 5 ALWAYS

In listening to someone else's lessons, can you readily identify the important points and isolate confusing or inappropriate ideas?

NEVER 1 2 3 4 5 ALWAYS

Do you find that body language, pauses, variations in voice tone are important parts of your communication style?

NEVER 1 2 3 4 5 ALWAYS

Do you believe it is particularly important for Christians to grow in knowledge of the Bible and what it means to be obedient to Christ?

NEVER 1 2 3 4 5 ALWAYS

In reading and researching, can you easily pull out basic ideas from initially unrelated material?

NEVER 1 2 3 4 5 ALWAYS

Is it easy for you to take Christian ideas and see how they apply in life situations?

NEVER 1 2 3 4 5 ALWAYS

Would you feel comfortable using a variety of learning methods in a class (i.e. lecture, experience, dialogue, visuals, role-playing, small groups)?

NEVER 1 2 3 4 5 ALWAYS

Do you enjoy reading material about the art of teaching and how to be a better teacher?

NEVER 1 2 3 4 5 ALWAYS

Do you enjoy listening to a good teacher and observing the teaching style and techniques?

NEVER 1 2 3 4 5 ALWAYS

Do you feel comfortable being considered an authority?

NEVER 1 2 3 4 5 ALWAYS

Are you open to people disagreeing with the ideas you present?

NEVER 1 2 3 4 5 ALWAYS

Do you feel that you have something to share with other Christians?

NEVER 1 2 3 4 5 ALWAYS

Do you have a regular and significant prayer life?

NEVER 1 2 3 4 5 ALWAYS

Do you have a particular concern for others?

NEVER 1 2 3 4 5 ALWAYS

Do you have a burning desire to see new Christians grow spiritually in Christ?

NEVER 1 2 3 4 5 ALWAYS

Do you feel that you are growing in your own spiritual life?

NEVER 1 2 3 4 5 ALWAYS

philosophy of ministry and be used in harmony with God's unswerving purpose for His Church and His people—the redemption of lost mankind.[12]

In a previous book we noted that:

> You would misuse Christ's gifts if you used them solely for service of existing Christians. That is not why these gifts are given. As we see God's overwhelming concern for the salvation of people, we must assume that His gifts are given, at least in large part, that the lost may come to know him.[13]

This does not mean that some gifts, such as evangelism, are more important than others. It does mean that all gifts should be used toward the goal of reaching, winning, and incorporating lost people into the fellowship of Christ's Body—the Church. And they can be.

But creatively structuring a philosophy of spiritual gifts into a Sunday School is not an easy task. It may be the subject of an interesting twelve-week study, or the topic for a weekend retreat. But to take seriously the fact that each member has been given gifts for service, and then to discover and use those gifts, is a demanding undertaking. Yet the rewards are tremendous: spiritual growth of the members, greater involvement of large numbers of people, satisfaction and high morale, and above all . . . growth.

## FOOTNOTES

### CHAPTER EIGHT

1. George G. Hunter, *Finding the Way Forward* (Nashville: Discipleship Resources, 1980), p. 55.
2. *Discover Your Gifts* is a 30-minute color film which creatively introduces laity to the concept of spiritual gifts and encourages them to begin searching for their own gift. It is available for rent from most religious film libraries, or from Christian Communication, 150 S. Los Robles, Suite #600, Pasadena, CA 91101.
3. C. Peter Wagner, *Your Spiritual Gifts Can Help Your Church Grow* (Glendale: Regal, 1979), p. 42.
4. This list is taken from the Modified Houts Questionnaire, copyright 1978, Fuller Evangelistic Association, DCG. Used by permission.
5. C. Peter Wagner, op. cit., p. 127.
6. Waldo Werning, *Vision and Strategy for Church Growth* (Chicago: Moody Press, 1977), p. 39.
7. C. Peter Wagner, op. cit., pp. 69-70.
8. Ibid., pp. 113-116.
9. A fine spiritual gifts questionnaire, to either use or adapt, is the "Modified Houts Questionnaire" available from Christian Communication, 150 S. Los Robles, Suite #600, Pasadena, CA 91101.
10. An excellent self-study kit—*Spiritual Gifts for Building the Body*—which includes textbooks, cassette tapes, spiritual gift inventory test, and self-study guide is also available from Christian Communication (see above address).
11. Elmer Towns, *How to Grow an Effective Sunday School* (Denver: Accent Books, 1979), p. 126.
12. David L. Hocking, *The World's Greatest Church* (Long Beach: Grace Ministries, 1976), p. 138.
13. Donald A. McGavran and Win Arn, *How to Grow a Church* (Glendale: Regal, 1973), p. 36.

# EPILOGUE

Here is a true story that has changed thousands of lives . . . . It was first told by Russell Conwell, a clergyman in Philadelphia, in 1881. It later became a part of a lecture entitled "Acres of Diamonds" . . . a lecture which he delivered more than five thousand seven hundred times.

By giving this lecture, Conwell raised more than eight million dollars which he used to establish Temple University, a school to help poor and needy youth gain an education. This story affected him very deeply, just as it affected his audiences.

It was the factual account of a farmer in the mountains of Africa who owned a very large farm with orchards, grain fields and gardens. He was contented and a wealthy man—contented because he was wealthy, and wealthy because he was contented!

One day a visitor came to his farm and began to describe the millions being made by others discovering diamond mines. He described in vivid detail the beautiful stones looking like drops of "congealed sunlight;" how a handful of diamonds would purchase all the desires of the heart, and place his children on thrones around the world through the influence of his great wealth.

That night the farmer went to bed a poor man—not that he had lost anything. He was poor because he was discontented, and discontented because he feared he was poor. As the farmer lay on his bed thinking of wealth he said aloud: "I want a mine of diamonds." All night he lay awake thinking about diamonds. Early in the morning he sought out the stranger for directions to where these gleaming gems might be found, and was told that they were found in white sands between high mountains.

"I will go," said the farmer! So he sold his farm, left his family with a neighbor and went away in search of diamonds. He searched through mountains and valleys, through deserts and plains. At last, when his money was all spent, and he was in rags, wretchedness, and ruin, he stood on a bridge with swirling water below. This poor, afflicted, suffering man could not resist the awful temptation to cast himself into the water, where he sank beneath the dark surface, never to rise in this life again.

One day the man who had purchased the farm noticed a curious flash of light on the bank of a shallow stream running through the farm. He reached in and pulled out a black stone having an eye of light that reflected all the colors of the rainbow. He took the curious pebble into the house and left it on the mantel, then went on his way and forgot all about it.

Some days later the same stranger returned. When he saw that flash of light from the mantel, he rushed up to it and said, "Here is a diamond . . . here is a diamond!"

"No, no," said the owner, "this is not a diamond. It is just a stone I found out in my stream."

"It is a diamond," insisted the stranger.

Together they rushed to the stream and stirred up the white sands with their fingers. There they found other, more beautiful, more valuable diamonds than the first. Thus was discovered the diamond mine of Golconda, the most magnificent diamond mine in all the history of mankind.

The first farmer had owned literally *acres* of diamonds—for every acre, yes every shovelful of that old farm revealed the gleaming gems. Yet he had sold them for practically nothing, for money to look for diamonds elsewhere. Had he only taken time and expended the effort to know what diamonds look like in their rough state, and had he first explored the land he owned, he would have had the riches he sought . . . right under his own feet!

What affected Dr. Conwell and his listeners was the obvious fact that each of us, at this moment, is standing in the middle of his own "acres of diamonds"—if we have the wisdom, the vision, and the determination to explore our possibilities . . . our potential right where we are.

When you look closely at your Sunday School, can you see an occasional brilliant flash of light, reflecting the splendid potential that lies within? Can you see an organization that, with vision and determination, can be honed into a beautiful, gleaming gem?

The churches that *have* caught this new vision for their Sunday School and acted on it are indeed seeing their Sunday Schools become the major instruments for growth and outreach into their community. Growth, for the great majority of Sunday Schools in America today, is possible. It requires commitment, it requires a desire to grow, it takes hard work. And often it necessitates a *new vision* for seeing the lost people in your community coming into a meaningful, life-changing relationship with Christ through your Sunday School. This new vision, taken seriously as a priority by your Sunday School members and leaders, will result in dramatic and unprecedented new growth.

Look down at your feet. Brush away some of the sand. There! Did you see it? That flash of brilliant light? You're standing on acres of diamonds . . . and they're yours for the taking!

# INDEX

## A



## B



## C

## K



## L



## M



## N



## O



## P



## R